Pater Petar Ljubicic

This is the Time of Grace

**May we be converted, may we pray
and may we believe in God!**

Medjugorje, 2006

This is the Time of Grace

Title of the original:

P. Petar Ljubicic

**"Vrijeme je milosti:
obracajmo se i vjerujmo
molimo i klanjajmo se Isusu!"**

translated from the German by

Mary Ann Fisher

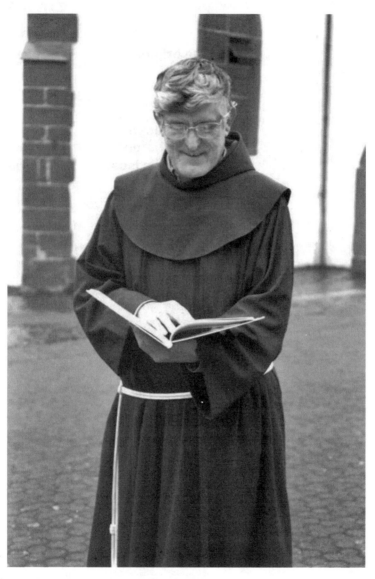

Father Petar Ljubicic

This is the Time of Grace

Through Mary to Jesus!

**With Christ and in Christ,
through life into eternity!**

**"If you knew how much I love you,
you would weep for joy!"**
(Queen of Peace)

**Lord of mercy,
Grant me Your grace,
That I may truly come to know You,
That I may have complete faith in You,
That each day I may love You fervently,
That I may serve You each day with my whole being,
That I may live in You and for You,
So that I may turn each moment of my life
Into a moment of salvation
For myself and others!**

You are loved by eternal love!

Find...

time for prayer, which is a great power on earth,
time for reflection, which is a source of strength,
time for friendship, which is a way to happiness,
time to love others, which is a great gift of God,
time to work, which is the price of success,
time for grace, which is the key to Heaven,
time for giving, which is victory over selfishness,
time for reading, which is the source of wisdom,
time to play, which is the secret of youth,
time for humour, which is balsam for the soul.

"Heavenly Father, I ask You
neither for good health nor for ill health,
neither for life nor for death,
only that You might determine
my health and my ill health,
my life and my death,
for Your honour, for my salvation!

You, the one and only God,
know what is beneficial for me.
You are the one and only Lord
and You do as You wish.
Give to me or take from me,
it is of no importance,
only make my will,
Lord, one with Yours!"
(Blaise Pascal)

This is the Time of Grace

CONTENTS

PART THREE 157

PART FOUR 203

Appendix.................................... 243

10

Alternative to a Preface

To write about Medjugorje presupposes belief in a mighty example of the intervention of God. It is the most significant event of last century. Some are even inclined to say that, because of their special nature, the apparitions in Medjugorje constitute the greatest event since the first Whitsun.

The first Whitsun marks the birth of the Christian Church. All those who were gathered together in prayer experienced the power and strength of the Holy Spirit. Over three thousand people asked the apostles what to do. The apostles replied that they should be converted and then be baptised. The people accepted this advice joyfully and acted on it.

The event of Whitsun is still going on today. Up until yesterday, as it were, the little village of Bijakovici was completely unknown; then Medjugorje became one of the best known places to which pilgrims come from all parts of the globe. They come with their problems, needs, sufferings and longings.

Many of them declare that in Medjugorje they found what they had been looking for: peace in their soul and true joy, genuine consolation and happiness.... Is this not what a person needs nowadays most of all?!

The power of the grace of God is so strong in Medjugorje that it becomes very evident in the numerous reports of conversions and miraculous healings in body and soul.

Over 20 million pilgrims have been to Medjugorje to date. Numerous books have been written on this world-renowned phenomenon. Various magazines are being published, to help us interpret and understand the messages from Heaven correctly.

Many people return there and say they cannot imagine their present spiritual life or convictions or total transformation without Medjugorje. Who can count all the people who say they spent the loveliest days of their life in Medjugorje? Many find it difficult to leave Medjugorje and the Queen of Peace, saying that part of their life remains there.

"In Medjugorje I found the peace I was searching for all my life!" (Branimir)

"I learned to pray with my heart in the place where Our Lady is!" (Marcel)

"On the Mount of Apparitions, I implored God and I experienced His proximity and His love!" (Patrik)

"I was never able to forgive. Since going to Confession in Medjugorje, I have obtained this grace and now I can forgive easily!" (Mario)

"I can confess better in Medjugorje than anywhere; there I can pour out my heart to God so easily, without being afraid or ashamed, so that I can tell Him anything!" (Kay)

"Since going to Medjugorje I do not swear any more and I go to church every Sunday!" (Felix)

"Medjugorje is where I first discovered what Holy Mass is and how much Jesus loves us!" (Kristina)

"I come to Medjugorje filled with joy and repeatedly receive the strength to win spiritual victories more easily!" (Paul)

A young pilgrim had just returned home from Medjugorje and was asked by her mother, "Did you see Our Lady in Medjugorje?" Somewhat surprised by the question, though not disturbed by it, she answered:

"Mum, there are two mountains in Medjugorje, the Mount of Apparitions and the Mount of the Cross, a lovely big church and nothing more; yet in this 'nothingness' you can find everything! I climbed up the Mount of Apparitions and prayed there. I shall never forget this prayer. I found, for the first time in my life, that God hears my prayers, that He loves me and that He has a plan for us. That was my first experience of God. Mum, you know I have always prayed and gone to Holy Mass regularly. Now I have felt profoundly and forcefully that Jesus is my great brother. He became our brother out of love for me and for everyone. He was born for me, lived for me, suffered for me, carried the heavy cross to Calvary for me and died there. Is there any greater love than this? Certainly there is not! Why didn't I know this before now? You only need go to this place filled with grace and experience it all.

'Our Lady, the Queen of Peace, has come to that mountain, where Heaven has opened up. I felt that Our Lady is my Mother and that she appears for me. Words of gratitude constantly flowed from my heart: 'Thank you, Mother, for these moments, filled with grace and salvation! Now I can see it all clearly. You, Our Lady, have come here, to guide us all to your Son Jesus. Through Him we can have everything: joy and peace, love and happiness in life. Jesus, come into my life; starting from today, I wish to belong only to You! I ask You to help me to surrender entirely to You!' "

That is how this girl described the way she perceived Our Lady. Her encounter with Our Lady of Medjugorje was a remarkable, unforgettable experience for this young soul. Such encounters have a decisive, life-long influence.

Our Lady has come to Medjugorje and has been appearing for 25 years (since 24.6.1981), making 9,131 days by the 25 th anniversary.

Nowhere and never before in the history of humanity have there been such apparitions for such a long time. Six visionaries have had the good fortune to see Heaven open and to speak to our heavenly Mother.

Our Lady calls upon us tirelessly to be converted more and more every day. She wishes our whole life to be one single prayer; she wants us to believe unwaveringly in God, thus surrendering to her completely! She emphasizes that renunciation and fasting are necessary for spiritual growth. Conversion, faith, prayer and fasting are all in vain without reconciliation. Our Lady therefore wants us to go frequently to Confession. Holy Mass is the most exalted part of our Christian life; the believer's life is based on this mystery.

Our Lady has been repeating her urgent, motherly call for 25 years. According to her own words, she has stayed so long in order to help us to withstand the present-day temptations. She would like to obtain as many graces for our salvation as possible.

Anyone who earnestly accepts her appeals to us and who tries to live in accordance with them will find peace, true joy and happiness. That is what Our Lady wants to achieve through her apparitions. Therefore this is the most important time of our life. Let us make as good use of it as possible!

A pilgrim from America says, "I have been in Medjugorje for a week and these have been the best days of my life! I have found true peace and God's love here. God has been very near to me and I have felt His love. I have been able to pray as never in my life before. I shall never forget the confession I made here. I am very rich but what I have now found is something that I did not have before!"

A doctor from Milan named Gildo Spaziante says, "Medjugorje is a great gift from God to our era. My wish is that we all recognize this quickly and open our hearts to these graces in humility and simplicity. Let us help each other so that the better times come sooner!"

This doctor has studied the Medjugorje healings. He has now published three books on the extraordinary healings which are attributed to Medjugorje.

A doctor who examined the Medjugorje visionaries, Primo Martinuzzi, was so impressed that he decided to become a priest. Though engaged to be married, he spoke to his betrothed of his plan, ceased to practise medicine and studied theology. He says, "From the moment I heard of the apparitions, I believed in them. I cannot imagine my life and my work as a priest without Medjugorje. I share the opinion of other theologians and researchers into Marian phenomena, recognizing in Medjugorje the completion of the cycle that began with Lourdes and then Fatima."

He adds, "After years of temptations, struggles, sufferings and pain, I expect that the great anniversary year 2000 will be a time of return for many a lost son. They will ask especially for us priests, in order to talk to us. I would like to get to know Jesus. I need Mary! It is Medjugorje that has prepared us for the era of the great return to God."

There are some events relating to Medjugorje that are worth looking at in more detail. Their true significance was not apparent until after Our Lady's apparitions began.

The painter Vlado Falak is from the parish of Medjugorje and paints in oils in his leisure time. He once painted a picture of Our Lady who appeared floating over the church in Medjugorje. Nobody was surprised and nobody asked him where the idea came from.

After the apparitions began, Father Petar asked him personally about the picture. He said he did not think about it beforehand and the picture was a spontaneous creation. We cannot dismiss this as just a coincidence. For someone who believes in God, there is no coincidence. We know that the eternal, omnipotent creator guides us and has all things in hand.

A charismatic congress took place in Rome early in May 1981. One of those present was Father Tomislav Vlasic. He was deeply worried about the state of the faith in Croatia because, at that time, the communist party was in power. Over Croatia hung the dark cloud of the reign of

16

terror. He therefore asked the charismatic Emilio Tardif and others praying there to present the suffering Croatian people to our Saviour and to ask for an answer as to what could be done in this difficult situation.

Everyone was astounded at the answer to this prayer. Father Tardif finally gave us the following message: **"There is nothing at all to be afraid of! I am sending you my Mother!"** Two months later Our Lady appeared in Medjugorje.

The visionary Ivanka was sitting with some other girls in April 1981 by the path that leads up to the Mount of Apparitions. Ivanka's mother had died three days previously. Suddenly the girls saw a woman in a white robe about 200 metres away. Ivanka immediately said, "Look, that's my mother!"

The girls were surprised and went home feeling uneasy. The question now was: who was this lady in white? After the apparitions began, Our Lady told Vicka, who had also been present: "That was the sign before the great sign, i.e. the apparition before the apparitions."

During the first few months of the apparitions, one could observe some unusual phenomena, especially light above the Mount of Apparitions, the Mount of the Cross and the church. Numerous pilgrims and witnesses could discern the form of a lady instead of the cross on the Mount of the Cross, not just for a few minutes but for a long time.

Sometimes there were even signs such as the sun spinning; the word for 'peace' ('mir') in shining letters in the sky; a big fire on the Mount of Apparitions one evening, visible from far and wide, but which left no trace.

25. 6. 2006   Father Petar Ljubicic

This miracle photo was taken in Germany in 2005. H.B., a believer, and his young daughter had simply seen a nice sunset from the window of their home and he had decided to photograph it, not knowing this extraordinary image of Our Lady would also appear on the film.

PART ONE

**"This is eternal life, that they know Thee the only true God,
and Jesus Christ whom Thou hast sent."**
(John 17, 3)

**"Our only happiness on earth consists in loving God
and knowing He loves us!"**
(Jean-Marie Vianney)

**"Just as the day cannot be imagined without the sun,
the world cannot be imagined without Mary!"**
(Father Branimirus)

"When I think of God, I am so indescribably happy!"
(Haydn)

Let us Turn Every Moment of our Lives into a Moment of Salvation!

We are all invited to recognize the value of the present moment, full of saving grace, which God's providence has given us.

The third Christian millennium has begun. What a great gift of God's this is and what an extremely great grace it is to live in this era. It is true that every era is a time of grace and salvation in its own way. Everyone has the chance to do something useful for himself and for his brothers and sisters.

Many people complain that we are living in a time full of crises and unrest. They are right. A serious crisis is shattering all aspects of our life. Yet a crisis is not the same thing as our downfall. A crisis only means being summoned to look critically at ourselves, to think about our life and to decide on a different, good, safe path.

Everyone agrees: mankind has never been more uncertain, fearful, worried and discontented, sinful and unhealthy than today. He has never been in deeper trouble and in greater torment than today. Each of us has more or less discovered that sin cannot give him happiness. Indeed, we cannot buy happiness for ourselves through sin!

Many people are starving in a spiritual sense nowadays. Materially they have got everything. Nevertheless they are starving. They possess everything but complain about this life. Their heart is seeking something greater: true peace and real joy, spiritual contentedness and genuine happiness in life.

Let us, however, be glad that we are hearing more and more of young people who are becoming aware of their great inner void. They feel a great longing for permanent, eternal values. It sounds plain and simple but it is true and obvious that a person needs more to live on than bread and cake, cars, a job and a great career. Man has an immortal soul and this soul feels loneliness and emptiness, boredom, abandonment and fear.

The only one in whom a human being can put his trust and to whom he can give his life is **Jesus Christ**. He alone can satisfy our hunger and thirst for life and for truth.

Despite everything that surrounds us, all the mishaps and misfortunes, we can sense that something new and beautiful must come: a wonderful light, incredible joy, true freedom and genuine peace.

Let us rejoice in the life that we live and have. It is a gift from God. The being called a 'person' is something wonderful. It is the great, treasured pearl, which is invaluable, the crowning glory of everything created. Every person has a mind and his own free will, consciousness and a conscience, an immortal soul and grace to make him holy. These are noble gifts, through which we are the image of God.

None of us is here by chance. God has thought of us for all eternity. **We are loved by eternal love.** The eternal and good God, who created us, has His great plan for us. The only question is: **have I discovered the plan which God has for me and for you?** Are we able to trust that God can do wonderful things in any heart, so that hearts open fully and give themselves irrevocably to Him? The psalmist sings: "What is man, for you to think of him? You made him but little less than God, crowned him with splendour and glory." (Ps. 8, 4-5)

Our whole life long we must learn that our life consists of the joyful moments of victory and the painful moments of defeat. It is filled with light and shadow and there is a constant mixture of love and lovelessness, joy and sadness, happiness and unhappiness. Temptations and passions, weaknesses and need, distress and illnesses, emptiness and boredom all batter the ship of our life.

Sin is the worst storm that can lay hold of the feeble ship of our life. There are few people who do not experience any difficult days or long, dark nights in their lives. Some moments in our lives are so bitter that we wish we had never experienced them. Some moments are so happy and beautiful that we wish they would last for ever.

It is important to know that such a life has its value. And the latter is considerable! For each one of us, this vale of tears consists mainly of struggling, searching and the perfecting and correcting of the deficiencies of our human nature. This makes it all the more important for us to bring to the fore the one who is above all these things and who is the only one who can help us: it is Jesus Christ, the ideal and the joy of our life, as a blessed soul says.

Therefore it is necessary to get to know oneself better every day, in order to endure each of life's situations as well as possible. Although our life's journey often takes us through troubled and high waters, it is a consolation to us that our good Father is watching over us precisely in such troubled and high waters, He who loves us immeasurably, who has given us life and entrusted us with an immortal soul, so that we may attain eternal splendour.

God will also give us the necessary enlightenment and the necessary strength, so that we can withstand everything and can reach Him. He would certainly not just leave us to face life's struggle without first arming us with the weapons of the spirit. Without them, no spiritual life is possible; they are the gifts of the Holy Spirit, the graces of the Sacraments, the Holy Masses, the prayers....

Above all, it is necessary **to trust God completely, the one who is love, mercy and goodness itself.**

We should never give way to the abyss of darkness and depression: despair, distrust, despondency or sadness.

We must constantly learn to replace darkness with light and dejection with joy. To do this, though, we have to practise, so that we are always aware how we can swim through rough seas and how bitterness and strife become navigable. To achieve this, we must frequently withdraw to our room and turn our gaze away from everything that is earthly and passing.

If ever it was necessary to withdraw to a solitary place and collect our thoughts, it is today. Our soul and our body call for it.

Through withdrawal to one's own room, one's own little domain, one's hermitage, speaking to God in prayer, this unity with Him... the great truth is always revealed to us: we recognize the motivation for our acts and deeds more easily. We recognize more easily whether our words are, in our heart of hearts, really pure and good. We shall have to justify every single word before God one day. However, if we listen to the voice of our conscience, it will be easier for us to feel divine grace and let ourselves be led by it. Then, truly, nothing in this world can keep us away from the love for our dearest one - for Jesus - and the true source of a life rich in grace.

We are all more or less aware that there is no life without problems and difficulties. Saint Francis of Sales says: "There is no vocation without boredom and bitterness, suffering and disappointments.... Can we make an exception of those who have devoted themselves to the will of God completely? Everyone would like to exchange his situation in life with someone else. Married people would prefer not to be married and unmarried people would prefer to be married.

"Where does this general spiritual dissatisfaction come from, if not from a few renegades rebelling beyond all measure and starting from the false premise that the other person is better off than ourselves?!"

To be able to accept life as it is means truly to lead a life in great wisdom. The truth is that we are never allowed to be content with the situation in which we find ourselves. It is important to know how one can maintain one's inner peace and remain patient; and above all to leave the leadership to Him who is Lord over life, space and time.

We should never forget that the present moment is the most important moment of your life, mine and every individual's. Why? Because the past moments are gone and I can never bring them back. We cannot influence coming moments very much. Therefore it is best to concentrate on the present moment. **A great deal depends on this moment, maybe even our eternity?!**

Let us always remember that this day and the present moment were given to us for us to work in them on our eternity. Therefore it is necessary to use them as well as possible. This gift is so great, as is the grace of knowing this and realizing it every moment.

That means transforming indeed every moment of our lives into a moment of salvation for us and for our brothers and sisters.

God seeks us! We are important to Him! He needs me! He needs you and every individual person. He has an absolute right to do so. Therefore He has also given us so many graces. Not everybody, though, is granted understanding of this. We are all obliged to endeavour to glorify God with our life. The only question is: how and where can we do so best and to the greatest advantage, most easily and surely?

Christ has never had a greater chance with us than today. Many people are hungry for God. We need courageous, noble, brave and determined souls who serve Jesus with determination, in order to make it possible for Him to get to all those who are far away. Maybe you are the soul that God has been waiting for and whom He would like to entrust with great secrets? Let us help God in saving even more people!

Let us now look at a striking example that will help us comprehend this moment of grace and thus enable us to change every moment into a moment of salvation.

Tauler was a humble, devout priest. He had implored God again and again to show him the shortest way to perfection. He had prayed for this for eight years. One day, while he was praying, he heard a voice say, "Go outside and the man you see will show you the way you seek!" The priest obeyed but there was only a beggar on the steps, who looked like anything but someone who could show him the way to perfection, so he did not pay any further attention to him but just greeted him and wished him a good day.

"Thank you for the greeting," said the beggar, "but I cannot remember ever not having had a good day."

"Then I wish you as much good fortune in all the days to come !" replied the priest.

"Thank you but I don't know when I was ever unhappy;
I am always happy !"

The priest asked the beggar to explain this. He answered, "I always have a good day, because whatever I get is what I take through God's hands, like poverty, hunger and scorn. That is when I honour God, so that every day turns into a good day; it is not the bad day that brings us obstacles and difficulties but our impatience! I am happy because I know that nothing happens to us that God does not want; what God wants for me is the best thing. I am blissfully happy, as the will of God is my joy and my contentment. Everything God does makes me so happy that I am a thousand times happier about it than others ever can be when one of their wishes is fulfilled. Blissful is the man whose will is always fulfilled, down to the last detail."

How great will our happiness be in Heaven? What reward will God give to those who have remained faithful to Him? Saint Paul says, '... the eye has not seen it, the ear not heard it ... '

God takes care of us in various ways. He never leaves us alone, not even for a moment. He advises and guides us, consoles us and heaps His graces on us. If that were not the case, how could one understand what a poor man said who, as a war victim, had lost everything he owned: "God is really so good. He has never left me!"

"He has never left you?" he was asked. "Didn't you have to leave your house and everything you owned? Didn't you lose your family, even your children?"

"Yes, I did. However, I have never lost my God. He has always consoled me! "

We must never forget or lose our God; then He will comfort us always and everywhere. That way our dear Lord will always be with us and He will hear us. We all wish to be blissfully happy, yet we are never satisfied. Neither goods nor treasures nor good health are enough to make us happy. What is earthly simply cannot satisfy us!

To be able to find true happiness, only one thing is necessary, namely that we grasp just one truth: we must be convinced that God is always near, whatever may happen in life. God is always with you! He loves you! Our Lord Jesus Christ will one day also do for us what He promised Catherine of Siena: 'Think of me and I shall think of you!' This is a great comfort to us all!

Mary is our Powerful Advocate!

Saint John Don Bosco was preaching in the Church of the Virgin Mary in Turin. Suddenly he stopped and asked the question, "Which of you can say who Mary is?" Almost nobody dared to answer.

Someone said, **"Mary is the Mother of God."** She is the Mother of our Saviour Jesus Christ. She is our Mother, the Mother of the Church, the Mother of all Christians.

In a book for children there is a little story. It tells how Mary once asked Jesus, "Which of all works is the greatest? What is the most beautiful thing God ever created?" Jesus said nothing. Then He looked at His Mother and smiled. The Mother of God understood. She is the most beautiful of all beings. She is and will always be one of the greatest works of God. She is the beauty of all beauties. This is what Saint Gregory calls her.

Mary is the one with grace, that is, **filled with grace**. She is chosen for all eternity. She fulfilled and succeeded perfectly in all trials. She remained true and withstood all temptations and this way she maintained her flawlessness. Mary was not raised to the status of the highest woman, the one rich in grace, for her own sake but for the sake of Jesus Christ; thus she has the status of the most blessed of all humans. Her being chosen is in harmony with the whole work of salvation.

Mary found complete grace in God. She was totally receptive to Him. She put her whole life at His disposal and believed that everything God had promised her would be fulfilled. **"Rejoice, you who are filled with grace! God is with you!"** Never before had a voice from God greeted someone that way and none has ever done so since.

Even Mary wondered at this; the greeting surprised her and she was fearful. She was privileged to hear: **"Do not be afraid, Mary, for you have found favour with God!"**

Indeed, only Mary was filled with grace from the first moment of her life and her whole life was filled with holiness. The Lord was always with her. She was without sin from the beginning, having been spared original sin and chosen to be the Mother of Jesus. Mary stayed true to the call of God every moment of her life and put herself at God's disposal completely and unreservedly.

Only Mary was able to say, at that moment: **"Behold, I am the handmaid of the Lord!"** She always served the Lord, the good, never evil and sin. Therefore Mary is our hope, hope which is certain for us Christians in the world. In her we discover how our life should proceed, what plan God has for us, for each one of us....

The Blessed Virgin Mary was and has remained an example to us all of belief, trust and prayer on our pathway as followers of Christ. She calls us and encourages us, so that we do not tire as we go along the path of holiness to eternity.

God called Mary and she answered readily. She pronounced her great 'FIAT' **('Let it be done!')**. God has called us too from the moment of our Baptism. Each one of us has been 'called by our name' by God, who has also 'determined lovingly that we shall become His sons and daughters through Jesus Christ'. He has called us to come to know Him, to love Him; to discover the plan He has for us and realize it every moment of our life.

God was the centre of Mary's life and of her actions. Mary received total salvation and was raised up by God, that is, she reached fulfilment in God. We do not yet know what this fulfilment is like. We simply say: **'Mary was raised into Heaven.'**

Mary's assumption into Heaven also gives us an answer to our own life. We are also on the way to attaining this fulfilment. Our life has its goal and its valuable meaning. It is worth living for this, because this is perfect, eternal life in God. Through Mary we discover what course our life should take and what plan God has for us. We Christians can also hope that He who is risen will lead us into His dwellings after we have completed our pilgrimage on earth, as He promised us.

When God calls us to do His works, He first waits for us to agree. We manage to find the strength for an initial, enthusiastic 'So be it! ', but we tire on the way to **'Thy will be done!'**. Sometimes we are not in a position to carry out His will or we do not want to give up our previous plans; we go back to worldly plans. Sometimes we do not accept new demands (wishes) of God's, because we are afraid of losses.

Mary is the example to us of how we should stay true to God's call to the end, that is, true to our answer to God's call. We should renew our answer to God's call day by day, so that we remain steadfast in what we promised. This is especially important when we are in difficult circumstances which tend to lure us away from God's call.

Mary's 'Thy will be done!' has another practical meaning too for each one of us. Mary's wonderful answer speaks from our lips and our heart whenever we follow the will of God in our life. Such an answer is most important in the decisive moments of life, such as when young people choose their occupation, so that this choice may be made according to God's will; then one will have chosen according to one's capabilities.

30

This answer is important in later life too, when God's will is clear regarding a particular task, in that it appeals to our conscience. It is very significant again when we are carrying our cross, so that we do not revoke what we promised through fear. At such moments, Mary's firm and irrevocable 'Fiat!' ('Let it be done!') should strengthen us.

Mary was and is the first Christian woman, having given birth to Jesus. She bore Him for us. Her wish is that we, too, bear Jesus on. We must all follow Mary's example if we wish to bring Jesus Christ into this dismal and sinful era, the authentic Jesus Christ from the Gospels. This way there is hope that the world will be improved, by virtue of this very Gospel.

The false leader of this world, Satan, offers humanity the opposite of what is good. This way he entices people away from God, so that they live in the world without God. We are all more or less aware that there can be no transformation of the earth without a transformation of our hearts. We can see how the possibilities of sustaining life are increasing, yet human life is so easily destroyed, on the war fronts, through revolutions and through abortions.

We all feel the need to seek the true meaning of life. We all long to be happy we are alive; we long for total peace and happiness. That is our nature. We would not be what we are if this were not the case. The son of Mary, Jesus Christ, gives us true life. He alone has 'words of eternal Life'. He alone is that Life, for 'in Him is Life and the Life was the light of men'.

However: 'He came into His property, Yet His own people received Him not.'

How do we receive Jesus today? This is the era of great graces and prayer, the era of conversion and atonement. God is at work in a powerful way.

At the same time though, Satan is hard at work too. He leads us astray and confuses us, brings unrest and uncertainty and wants to destroy every plan of God's. We cannot help having the impression that the end of time has begun. Let us count on the fact that God is stronger than evil and stronger than everything we fear. It is very important that we are prepared when an invitation comes to us from Heaven.

An example: in Venice there is a church dedicated to Our Lady. Its name is 'Maria della salute!' ('Our Lady of Rescue!'). How did this name come into being? In the 16th century, the plague was rife in Europe. Death was merciless and claimed many victims. Then the inhabitants of Venice took a vow. They promised to build a church to the Queen of Peace, the help of Christendom, if she would save them from this epidemic. God heard their prayers with the Blessed Virgin Mary as their advocate. The Venetians fulfilled their vow and built a church. This is another sign that Our Lady hears our prayers when we supplicate her.

Why Does Our Lady Appear?

After a lecture, a colleague of mine, Felix, came over to me and said, "I am now going to tell you something that I normally tell virtually no-one. It is a wonderful thing to have a mother. I have no mother. She died for me."

"How did that happen?" I asked.

"She died so that I could live. It could not be both ways. Either I had to die in my mother's womb to let her stay alive or she had to die to save my life, my aunt told me later. My mother did not agree to my dying and so she died." This happened in Mosor, a small village on the Adriatic coast. This mother died voluntarily to save her child. She was a great, heroic mother.

We cannot imagine the world without a mother, both here in this world and in Heaven. God created us in such a way that we can not be happy without the mother who takes us by the hand and guides us. God therefore gave us our Mother, to spur us on.

We can find the answer to the question "Why does Our Lady appear?" in an unwritten law of providence. Mary comes to help us whenever times of danger to the Church arise or it is under threat or the world is in a crisis.

We should not forget what the visionary of Kerizin (a village in France's Britanny) heard during an apparition of Jesus: "When the people of this world rejected God, He sent Me, to bring humanity and the world back to Him. The world rejected Me too and then I sent my Mother into the world. She was sent here with a great task to perform. She is to be the mediator between Me and humanity. You cannot reach salvation without my Mother. I now dispense My graces through her; they are all given through her.

Humanity can no longer return to God without her. These times are particularly serious. The struggle between the light and the darkness is now paramount." (28.4.1958)

Mary became the Mother and remained the Mother. She thus became the mediator between Heaven and earth, between her Son Jesus Christ and the whole of humanity.

To us she is always a sure way to reach God. She became and remained our powerful intercessor in relation to her Son, because she takes on our cause like our own mother. Mary is therefore the hope of all who despair, the consolation of all who are sad, the health of all sick and weak people and the help of all sinners.

Our Lady has been appearing in the parish of Medjugorje for around twenty-five years. This is a great gift from Heaven. It is not only a gift for the congregation there and the Croatian people but for all of humanity. It is a great grace for everybody and one that virtually cannot be repeated.

Our Lady has come to visit us as the Queen of Peace. She has given us the tidings of peace. She shows us exactly how to attain peace in our hearts and in the world and also eternal peace in God.

Mary wishes to help us to be open to the spirit of the Gospel, so that we give first place in our life to God. This way we can gain eternal life. As our Mother, she tirelessly calls upon us to have strong, unwavering faith.

Jesus Christ is true God and true Man. He is our peace and our joy, our life and our salvation. His Gospel is the Glad Tidings of salvation for all humanity.

Mary never ceases to tell us we must be converted anew every day. She has called upon us countless times to pray with our heart. She calls upon us to do the following: to pray daily the Creed, seven Lord's Prayers, seven Hail Marys and seven Glory Be to the Fathers and also daily the Rosary. Besides, we should attend Holy Mass humbly and reverently and worship Jesus in the Most Holy Sacrament. It is her great wish that Holy Mass be our joy and our life. Every family should read the Holy Bible and pray together.

She does not fail to remind us to live her messages, i.e. to fast, preferably on bread and water, on Wednesdays and Fridays; to live at peace with God and our brothers and sisters; to go to Confession monthly. She wants to make us into true believers, genuine witnesses for Christ.

It is very clear from the messages of Our Lady that, of all worthwhile things, love and peace are the greatest and most necessary and that belief and prayer, conversion and fasting are vital conditions for their realization.

So that we find true peace, Mary has called upon us to have complete faith in God. **Faith** is a gift from God, which enables us to surrender our whole being to God. To believe in God is an act of total devotion. This means that God is given first place in our life and that we place all our hope in Him and live entirely for Him.

Without genuine **conversion**, living faith is impossible. Conversion is a grace, through which we recognize God and become witnesses of His love and of His great plan for us. To be converted means to have experienced God's existence and to be humble before Him, to acknowledge our sins before Him and also to repent of them.

To be converted means to live a new life, to see everything in a new light, to change and to help others so that they can change too. This is all brought about through the grace of God, which a person becomes receptive to and through which he lives. To be converted means to become more upright, more just, nearer to perfection and holier day by day. This is a task for our whole life.

Fundamental, profound and lasting conversion is unthinkable without **prayer**. Mary has repeated her calls to prayer countless times.

Prayer is the heart and soul of our faith, our conversion and our peace. Prayer is, however, also a gift from God. Man has a deep longing to be with God, to speak to Him and to live in unity with Him.

Prayer is thus the breath of the soul. Our Lady says, "Be aware, my dear ones, that I am your Mother and that I have come to earth to teach you to obey out of love, to pray out of love..." (29.11.1984) In joyful devotion to God in prayer, we experience His love most strongly and that way we too will love Him.

Our Lady wishes ardently that we **pray with our heart**, i.e. not out of habit and also not because it is customary. To pray with one's heart means to pray with love, with one's whole being and with body and soul, i.e. to be completely receptive to Him, to devote oneself to Him with trust, to place all one's hope in Him, to put Him first in our life, i.e. to pray with concentration and humility, devotion and trust, reverence and piety. According to Our Lady's messages, prayer with the heart is like a joyful encounter with God.

So that we can remain on the path of faith, conversion and prayer, we have to be prepared to practise renunciation. **We should fast!** "Through fasting, a person comes to believe. Through it he becomes constantly stronger inwardly and thus gains assuredness in self-control. Only he who has power over himself can become free and capable of devoting his life to God and other people, as the faith requires." (Dr Ljudevit Rupcic)

"Dear children, ... above all, fast, for through fasting you will cause the whole plan of God here in Medjugorje to be realized and you will give me joy ..." (26.9.1985)

the visionaries in ecstasy

Jakov, Ivan and Marija during an apparition

Convert Every Day!

To be converted means to know that God exists and to recognize that He is the most important thing in our lives. That is to say, the life of a person becomes meaningful only when he lives in harmony with the plan God has for him. Part of this plan is that the person comes to know God, loves Him with his whole being, devotes himself completely to Him, serves Him joyfully and thereby becomes perfect and holy. God then fills the heart of the person with perfect joy, genuine peace and spiritual satisfaction. The person feels he is saved.

This is the Time of Grace

One could say that conversion is a feeling of grace, a feeling that God is here, that He loves me and wants to make me happy for eternity. Conversion also means, however, being constantly in search of God. It means returning to God; admitting all one's mistakes and all one's sins; renouncing evil and all sinful tendencies. When we are converted and we repent of all our sins, we obtain the grace to change, to become better, more just, more upright, more honest, nearer to perfection and holiness.

We are invited to convert every day, every moment and to become more and more attached to God with our whole heart and our whole being. Conversion is the basic message of the New Testament. The Gospel according to St Mark begins directly with an appeal to be converted: "The time has been fulfilled; the Kingdom of God is near at hand. Be converted and believe in the Gospel!" (Mark 1,15)

Conversion is the prerequisite for any spiritual life and for holiness. Without conversion, there is neither spiritual growth nor holiness; there is neither true faith nor genuine love. When we grasp that the essential thing in conversion is the recognition that we are dependent on God, then we will also grasp that conversion is not something we experience only once but is a process that continues our whole life.

We are called upon to be converted and this echoes constantly in our ears. Here one must ask oneself: "Am I taking this seriously? Does this make me want to change my life so that I become similar to Jesus?" It means we must repeatedly be converted anew, which entails a new attitude to life; every moment we must ask ourselves what place God occupies in our life and what He means to us.

We are all tempted at times to ask when the process of conversion will finally be over and when we can, as Christians, finally relax, throw away our cross and enjoy this life. This is a temptation which would bring the process of our conversion to a halt; our conversion is never complete; our spiritual efforts must continue and never tire; the example that was set us for our life is Jesus and His perfection.

It is necessary to be 'rapt in Jesus Christ', as St Paul says. Therefore it is necessary for everyone to encounter Jesus; everyone must go on his own 'path to Damascus'. Jesus reveals His light, goodness and love to all those who seek Him with sincere belief and a contrite heart. He gives us the grace that enables us to start out for a new life.

From the moment at which a person becomes rapt in Jesus Christ, everything else loses its value. Nothing counts any more except Jesus: one's habits, comforts, career, or enjoyment of any kind. The follower is prepared to let go of all that, to walk closely with Jesus, so as to become like Him. Only such a Christian can live his true identity: a Christian is like a second Christ.

A true, upright, converted Christian who is rapt in Jesus Christ conducts his life similarly to Jesus, that is, he will be filled with grace and prepared to forgive, knowing that, as a person, he is weak; he is only strong and great in Jesus.

Jesus therefore calls on us constantly to be converted. He even says, "You too will all perish, if you are not converted." (Luke 13,5) This really is a serious warning! Jesus is not joking. Time passes quickly and eternity is approaching. Let us keep this in mind! We all are often deceiving ourselves when we think we have time. It is not clever to postpone one's conversion and shut one's ears to God's call. We must not try God's patience.

Conversion is the grace that helps us to live always with God. Grace is what comes before the call of God. Conversion is the repentant answer of the heart to the call of God, the impulse being grace. To be converted is to answer the call of God with one's whole being and thus to make the right choice, i.e. to steer one's life in the direction that Jesus planned for it.

This means freeing oneself from all the attractions of the worldly things which would like to take us prisoner here and now. It is right to be converted to God. It means breaking the chains that have no value: glory, envy, the enticement of things that are not worthwhile and of wealth gained quickly. Jesus generously pursues the wish to fulfil the will of God with regard to everyone. To be converted means to fulfil the promise of one's Baptism: to renounce sin and lead the life of a child of God.

Even though conversion is a grace, it requires a lot of effort and suffering. We must undergo renewal in the depths of our heart and then start changing inwardly. Daily effort is needed on our part. It is of eternal value and is the sign and hallmark of our love of God, showing that we love Him above all else and that we love our brothers and sisters and serve them.

Let us not forget the Christian message of great importance, namely that God approached man through His embodiment in Jesus Christ. Jesus loved us so much that He took all our weaknesses and sins upon Himself and made restitution to God for them through His death on the cross. He rose from the dead on the third day and, in so doing, He triumphed over all death, all torment, all sin and all evil. Thus everyone who is converted and believes in this truth goes from death into life. He lives eternally.

A girl, asked what she would say about conversion, answered: "Conversion, to me, is a gift, a grace, a joyous encounter with the living God. It is a profound experience, a spiritual experience, in which I completely open my heart to God and it is imbued with His light, His love and His graciousness. I am united with God. That was the moment of grace when I realized that God loves me, that He is my friend and that He has His plan for me.

'To be converted means to me to allow Jesus to come to me and envelop me totally in the power of His grace. This means surrendering myself fully to Him, putting my whole life in His hands and praying that He take upon Himself all my sins, all the weaknesses, the sinful habits and all the wounds of my soul.

'To be converted means precisely to realize that Jesus is an ocean of love and the Bread of Life; He is true happiness, unmarred joy and real life, which I long for with every fibre of my heart. From this moment on I fear nothing, for He is with me. This is as certain as my spiritual rebirth. I feel I have been given new eyes, new hands, a new heart....

'To sum it up, one could say: 'Come, Lord, so that I may place myself completely in Your hands; whatever You wish for me, let it be done!' "

Mihaly Szentmartoni, in his book **Searching for Fulfilment** (pp. 23-9), discusses the process of conversion as taking place in four phases:

the initial crisis (an unpleasant feeling, uncertainty, discontent);

the recognition that there is someone with us who is taking care of us (God the Father, providence, the goodness of God);

the recognition of a new truth (seeing everything in a new light);

the joyous release (the feeling of relief, salvation, joy, rejoicing).

All this is very evident in the example of the conversion of the English cardinal John Henry Newman. He was born in London in 1801. After his studies, he became an Anglican cleric and served in a small church in Oxford. There he also held church services. From the start he was a true and correct Anglican believer but, searching through the texts of the fathers of the Church, he found his soul increasingly in doubt.

Finally, in 1845, Newman converted to the Catholic faith, after a great deal of reflection and correspondence with people who thought as he did. Later he became a priest and the Pope even made him a cardinal. He died in Birmingham in 1890. He has left us a great many writings. Newman's beatification is being pursued.

Let us now look at the four phases of the conversion of Cardinal Newman as described in his own words.

The initial crisis: every conversion is preceded by an unpleasant feeling in the soul, like dissatisfaction, uncertainty, uneasiness, a feeling of unhappiness, abandonment or insufficient understanding. These are all signals that help us to take stock of our life so far. It occurs to us that something is wrong with us. Our life is not as it should be. We are then in a crisis.

The critical moment in the life of John Henry Newman came on a voyage to Sicily, where he fell seriously ill. He had to take to his bed for several days and there was no doctor nearby to help him. Depressed as he was through high temperatures and so helpless, he became aware of what state his soul was in. The man accompanying Newman thought he was going to die and suggested he make his will. Newman's answer was to become famous: "No, I am not going to die; I have not sinned against the Light and, besides, I have a mission to fulfil in England!"

Being aware of the existence of God, who accompanies us with His love: awareness of the presence of the one and only God as our Father and His providence is really important. It means being aware of godly grace, which helps us to understand that we are forgiven for everything and that we are loved and absolved, i.e. saved.

John Henry Newman emerged from his state of illness as a completely new person. He left Palermo and boarded a ship bound for Marseille. The ship could not put to sea because there was no wind. While waiting to set off he thought about his life and how wonderful providence had been to him in the past. These reflections bore fruit in the form of a beautiful hymn, still sung today by the English in church:

The Pillar of the Cloud

Lead, Kindly Light, amid the encircling gloom,
Lead Thou me on!
The night is dark, and I am far from home,
Lead Thou me on!

This is the Time of Grace

Keep Thou my feet; I do not ask to see
The distant scene; one step enough for me.

I was not ever thus, nor pray'd that Thou
Shouldst lead me on.
I loved to choose and see my path; but now
Lead Thou me on!
I loved the garish day, and spite of fears,
Pride ruled my will; remember not past years.

So long Thy power hath blest me, sure it still
Will lead me on,
O'er moor and fen, o'er crag and torrent, till
The night is gone;
And with the morn, those angel faces smile
Which I have loved long since, and lost awhile.

(J.H. Newman)

The discovery of a new truth: the third phase in the process of conversion is new enlightenment. The person becomes aware of a truth he had forgotten. New values are discovered. Secrets of our life are understood or at least accepted.

Newman had been brought up in the Anglican faith and had a good many prejudices with regard to the Catholic faith and its devotions. One of the truths of our faith which he had not been able to understand was our devotion to the Blessed Virgin. He writes of his inability to accept the idea that the Catholics appeal to Mary as an attorney and a mediator of all graces: "From my childhood I was taught that there is no mediator between a soul and God and this is how I lived my spiritual life. I always thought this piety regarding Mary was in line with the Mediterranean mentality but not the English. I always stood before my Creator and the mediator was only Jesus Christ. Now, however, I know that Mary is not the mediator as I saw it but a way to God."

A feeling of certainty came into his soul, so that he thankfully wrote: "I am never fearful as to whether my new path is right or not."

Joyfulness: the fourth and final phase of the process of conversion is described as an experience of freedom, joy and the awareness that we are loved. This is the joy of salvation, the joy of a person who knows he is in the state of grace.

Newman really did experience ecstasy at the moment he became Catholic. The following written account of that moment has been passed down to us: "From the moment I became Catholic, I have had, of course, nothing further to report on the development of my thoughts on the subject of faith. By that I do not mean my spirit was passive or I stopped reflecting on the truths of the faith. I mean I have no fear of any kind left in my heart. I am glad to live in perfect peace without any doubts."

Have Unwavering Faith in God!

The father of a certain family had no faith. The mother, however, was a true believer. They had a daughter aged sixteen, who oscillated between the mother who believed and the unbelieving father. The mother went to church regularly but the father just laughed about it all.

The daughter loved both her father and her mother. One evening, these parents were standing at their daughter's bedside and the girl realized that her parents were afraid

46

she could die soon. While her father stood on one side of her bed and her mother on the other, the girl took her father's hand and her mother's hand and asked, with despair in her voice: "If I now had to die, how would I die, in my father's unbelief or in my mother's faith?" The father began to weep, leaned over his daughter and said to her, "My child, die in your mother's faith, for my lack of faith is worthless!" The girl listened to her father and asked God for the gift of faith that her mother had.

The gift of belief comes from God and is undeserved. It helps us to grasp that we come from God, we belong to Him and we shall go to Him one day. Believing is an act of total trust and conscious devotion to Jesus Christ personally, who loves us. To believe means to accept Christ, who died and rose again, as one's own way, truth and life. This means having peace, joy, happiness and salvation in Jesus.

To believe means to be absolutely convinced that God exists, that He loves us ardently, that He has His definite plan for us; this entails having total trust in Him. When one believes in God truly and unwaveringly, one is always open and humble before Him. One thinks of God as something of the greatest value. One is always willing to listen to Him; one places all one's trust and hope in Him. God reveals Himself to us in the person of Jesus Christ. Jesus says: "Whosoever believes has eternal life...." and "For it is the will of my Father that all those who see the Son and believe in Him shall have eternal life." (John 6, 47 & 40)

Dr Tomislav Ivancic writes: "In theology we speak of three levels in belief: believing in God; believing God; believing into God."

'Believing in God' means believing that He exists. This is not a decision in favour of faith (or not necessarily one). If it is, then it is only an initial decision; someone who believes in the existence of God does not automatically act as a believer.

'Believing God' means believing in the truth of everything that God has said, prophesied or promised. This is belief in the mind, the intellect. A person can agree in his mind with the truth of Jesus without living in accordance with this truth. What is lacking in him is belief in this truth with his heart as well.

'Believing into God' means placing one's existence in God's hands; it means 'leaping' into what Jesus gave us; relying on the words of Jesus and being a follower; surrendering one's life to Jesus Christ. This is a process of trust in the person Jesus, on the one hand, and of complete confidence that He will keep all His promises, on the other hand. Thus it is a matter of belief that is trusting and belief that is confident. The first one relies on the person Himself and the second one on His promises. Here, belief approaches hope and love.

"One who is confident is one who hopes; one who trusts is one who also loves. Belief, hope and love go hand in hand. The more one matures in one's belief, the more one grows in the matter of love too, which involves longing to be united. This is essentially a longing for union with God in eternity." (Dr Tomislav Ivancic, Encountering the Living God, p. 133)

Belief is the most valuable treasure in this world. It is an invaluable gift and must therefore be prayed for. One must guard this belief as one does one's sight and one's soul.

The Queen of Peace calls upon us tirelessly to have strong faith:

The Queen of Peace came to us, her children, to help us and to lead us to God. She does this like a true mother, who wants the best thing for her children. Therefore, the first thing that she wishes is that we believe she was sent by her Son to help us with our problems, difficulties and in this great crisis in which all of humanity finds itself.

Our Lady herself says she came "to awaken the belief of every believer". (30 4.1984)

"When you are far from God, you cannot receive graces because you do not seek them with a firm faith. Day by day, I am praying for you, and I want to draw you ever more near to God, but I cannot if you don't want it. Therefore, dear children put your life in God's hands." (25.1.1988)

"Therefore, little children, believe and pray that the Father increase your faith, and then ask for whatever you need. I am with you and I am rejoicing because of your conversion." (25.4.1988)

Her caring, motherly call to pray and to be open to the Holy Spirit is meant to strengthen our belief in particular. "Dear children! These days I call you especially to open your hearts to the Holy Spirit. Especially during these days the Holy Spirit is working through you. Open your hearts and surrender your life to Jesus so that He works through your hearts and strengthens you in faith. Thank you for having responded to my call." (23.5.1985)

"Dear children! Today I wish to say to everyone in the parish to pray in a special way to the Holy Spirit for enlightenment. From today God wishes to test the parish in a special way in order that He might strengthen it in faith. Thank you for having responded to my call." (11.4.1985)

"Today I want to call all of you to decide for Paradise. The way is difficult for those who have not decided for God. Dear children, decide and believe that God is offering Himself to you in His fullness. You are invited and you need to answer the call of the Father, Who is calling you through me." (25.10.1987)

"I am with you and I want you to believe me, that I love you." (25.11.1987)

In Medjugorje, a young man and his sister found faith:

A girl tells us how she lived without faith and without God from the age of 15 to 20 years. She loved the things all young people love: staying out late, discos, rock concerts and friends. She admits that this only gave her temporary happiness and that afterwards she was filled with great emptiness and uneasiness. She suffered greatly from this. She longed for real happiness and real joy.

The girl's mother was a devout and exemplary Catholic. One day her mother perceived, during prayer, that Our Lady said, "Make a pilgrimage to Medjugorje!" "That was a sign that my mother was praying for me, my brother and my father, since we were not believers. When she told us she wanted to take us for a pilgrimage to the Queen of Peace in Medjugorje, we refused and we even argued. I thought, 'What am I supposed to do there? Maybe it is true that Our Lady is appearing there and helping a lot of people. Maybe all sorts of people could be converted there and start to believe, but I certainly could not!' Then came Good Friday, 1990, which I shall never forget. There was an apparition on the Mount of

50 This is the Time of Grace

the Cross. During the apparition I felt very strongly that Our Lady was present. I could not see her with my own eyes but in my heart I felt she was my Mother who had guided me there. I could grasp that God was present. I was granted the gift of belief. I understood that God loves me and that He is my creator.

'I know it is very hard to sum up such an experience in words, for the words of this world are inadequate for this. Such experiences are quite extraordinary: belief, God,....We can live a long, long time on such experiences.

'After experiencing all this, I went to Confession. I must say all this was like a shock to me: to realize that God exists, that He loves me and to confess to Jesus, who has become my great brother. I also immediately decided to live the messages that Jesus sends us through His Mother. The messages also helped me to understand that Mary leads me to her Son Jesus. Gradually there arose in my heart the wish to surrender my whole life to Jesus. One day I prayed for the strength to do this, but where was I to begin? After three weeks I decided for the Community of the Beatitudes."

This girl declares she has found the true way to happiness. The joy the Lord has now given her is far greater than the one she knew before. She also told of how her brother was converted. "In Medjugorje he met a lot of young people. He felt in his heart that he should go to Confession. Then during Holy Communion he felt, deep in his heart, the presence of Jesus. He prayed, then kneeled down and thanked God for this gift." It was her brother's moment of conversion.

When he arrived home, however, he fell into his old ways again and lived as before his conversion. His sister says,

"My mother and I prayed a lot for him. Then, when he went on another pilgrimage to Medjugorje, God restored to him the grace of conversion that he had lost. This was his ultimate conversion. He now lives the messages of Our Lady every day, has entered the Community of the Beatitudes and wants to become a priest."

This shows how the prayer of Our Lady of Medjugorje helped this family find God; they also have the charisma of true, delightful unity.

pilgrims praying on the Mount of the Cross

Pray with your Heart!

Prayer is a joyful encounter with God, who loves us so much and always has time to listen to us. He is always waiting for us. Prayer is a fond exchange between God and the person. Everyone longs for God, longs to unite with God in His love and find peace, joy and life's happiness in Him. Prayer is therefore a joyful union between God and a person in the light of belief, hope and love.

Prayer is and always was an expression of the deepest need of the human soul: it is the search for God. This is the fundamental nature of the soul. It wants to worship God as its creator and honour Him; it wants to show Him its devotion and love. It wants to thank Him for the gifts it has received and make up for sins it has committed.

Prayer entails becoming aware of one's limits and weaknesses, uncertainties and helplessness, in order to ask for help from the almighty Father. This means creating an environment for ourselves in which we can ask God for the strength to make ourselves holy, to purify, strengthen and encourage ourselves and thus help ourselves along our life's path.

Praying means that we free ourselves from everything we are dependent on, in order to find time to be alone with God and to speak with Him as with the Father who loves us and is waiting to console us and make us joyful. It is sweet union with God, in trust and love. Praying means being aware and firmly believing that we can speak with God, that we can unite with Him and that we are one with Him in His love.

Is there anything more beautiful, better, more necessary, more useful, more wholesome and more human for a person to do than kneel down, fold one's hands and then express one's faithfulness and devotion, one's love and gratitude for the goodness one has received? That means praying and, in prayer, feeling and perceiving great joy and great happiness. A true and genuine believer knows that his soul cannot live without prayer. Therefore one need not tell him anything about the necessity of prayer.

The question of how we should pray nowadays:

We should pray with our heart. Our Lady has been teaching us this for more than 24 years. What does this mean? It means that we should not pray out of habit or because it is customary to pray.

To pray with one's heart means above all to pray with love, with all one's soul, with all one's being and with a pure heart. This in turn means to be completely open to God, to give Him first place in our life, to have absolute faith in Him and to hope for everything that is good from Him. It means to concentrate, to be humble, devoted, filled with faith, reverent and persevering.

According to the indications and the messages of Our Lady, prayer with our heart is also a prayer experience. It is an encounter with God. It means to unite with Jesus and experience the beauty and the greatness of the grace which God has given us. It also means to receive great graces. To pray with our heart means to leave all obstacles for God to remove. Prayer should predominate in our heart at all times. God hears every prayer.

Not infrequently we hear someone say something like: "I wanted this or that from God but He did not hear my

This is the Time of Grace

prayer. I prayed for the health of my father or mother or children but He did nothing! I prayed that I would pass my exam but I failed it. If God heard my call for help, why did He not give me a response accordingly? If God is a God of love and goodness, why does He not show this and grant my request, which is justified?" Such reproaches are widespread. What can we say to them?

Many people think that God is like a service or a kind of rescue squad and that, when we want something, He must meet our requirements. We then pray e.g. the Lord's Prayer and the Hail Mary or we buy a Holy Mass and God is supposed to give us what we require of Him, as with a kind of self-service business.

Have we ever asked ourselves why God did not grant the request we prayed for? Maybe we only remember Him when we need something special or when we or our folk are sick or when we are not strong enough ourselves to achieve what we want. Otherwise we do not bother with God or prayer. Do we really ask ourselves if what we want from God is good for us and our soul? Maybe it is dangerous for us; could it lead to our destruction? It could also be the case that, when we prayed, we were in a state of serious sin or we were proud. Did we think about this? Perhaps God did not give us what we prayed for but something else instead.

So many people pray for their health, yet God did not give them healing but the strength to bear their illness patiently. Perhaps God did not grant us what we asked for in prayer because we wanted Him to do our will and not His. When we ask God for something, our prayer must be filled with devotion to Him and end with 'but not as I wish, rather as You wish'. (Matt. 26, 39)

Lastly, even if it seems that our prayer was not heard, in fact it was indeed heard, for His will was done and not ours. If He did not give us what we wanted, it was only because He knows better what is necessary for our eternal well-being.

Under what conditions does God grant what we pray for? One point is clear: God is prepared to hear all our prayers. Even before we ask Him for something, He knows what we need. The Holy Scriptures confirm this: 'Call to me and I will answer you and tell you great, hidden things, which you do not know.' (Jer. 33, 3) 'Ask and it will be given you; seek and you will find; knock and it will be opened to you. For everyone who asks, receives; he who seeks, finds; and, to him who knocks, it will be opened.' (Matt. 7, 7-8)

It is important to remember that God is omniscient and omnipotent. He knows everything and He can do everything. St Paul emphasizes the omnipotence of God when he writes: 'He who, by the power at work within us, is able to do far more abundantly than all that we ask or think ...'. (Eph. 3, 20)

So that what we pray for can be granted, we must fulfil certain conditions: Above all we need **strong faith.** 'And whatever you ask in prayer, you will receive, if you have faith.' (Matt. 21, 22) We must believe that God can give us everything we ask of Him in prayer. 'Without faith it is impossible to please (God); for whoever would draw near to God must believe that He exists and that He rewards those who seek Him.' (Heb. 11, 6)

It is necessary that **our heart be pure** when we pray. This is a very important condition. If we are in a state of serious sin, God does not grant what we pray for, because through our sin we have lost access to His grace. That way, moreover, we have no merit before God.

For God to grant what we pray for, we must remove all obstacles. It is absolutely necessary to refrain from sin, to repent of one's sins totally and to admit them at Confession. When we decide to avoid sin in future, God forgives us joyfully and restores to us the grace that we lost through our own fault.

It is important **to live in unity with God.** This unity becomes evident when we are seeking and fulfilling the will of God. It is the will of God that we be totally open to the Holy Spirit, so that the Spirit can guide us and carry out the works in us that are necessary for our salvation. Jesus says: 'If you abide in Me and My words abide in you, ask whatever you will and it shall be done for you.' (John 15, 7)

Jesus prayed in Gethsemane: 'My Father, if it be possible, let this cup pass from Me; nevertheless, not as I wish but as You wish.' (Matt. 26, 39) To trust in God and ask that His will be done regarding us and those for whom we pray is the best condition for having God grant what we pray for.

For God to grant what we pray for, it is necessary **to thank God** for everything. We can pray as follows, 'Lord, thank You for the grace of being able to ask for what is needed. You know better than I do what I need for my well-being and for my eternal salvation. The same applies to my brothers and sisters.' The Scriptures say: 'Have no anxiety about anything but in everything by prayer and supplication with thanksgiving let your requests be made known to God.' (Phil. 4, 6)

It is very important for us **to be patient.** When we wish for something from God, we want Him to give us everything immediately. In so doing, we keep forgetting that we do not know what is best for us at this moment. This is why it is necessary to be very patient and to leave everything to God, for Him to decide when He will fulfil our requests. If God gave us everything we want at the moment we ask Him for it, we would certainly be disappointed with the result. We ourselves are greatly limited, concerning our future in particular. We cannot know what is to be. Therefore it really is best to leave everything to God.

We should make all our requests in the name of our Lord Jesus Christ, who said: 'Whatever you ask in My name, I will do it, that the Father may be glorified in the Son; if you ask anything in My name, I will do it.' (John 14, 13-14)

Let us also not forget to thank God in our prayers and to honour and glorify Him through our prayers. Let us strive for justice, love and peace, i.e. for the Kingdom of God or, better, for the will of God. Then we shall receive from God whatever we ask; for if we have fulfilled all the requirements God has set down for us, He will not be able to refuse us anything at all.

We learn from St Paul:

In his second letter to the Corinthians, St Paul describes his experience of revelation, when he was in the third Heaven. One cannot describe in words what he saw and experienced in Paradise. In his first letter to the Corinthians, he says: 'As it is written in the Scripture, we tell of what no eye has seen, nor ear heard, nor the heart of man conceived, the greatness of what God has prepared for those who love Him.' (1 Cor. 2, 9)

58   This is the Time of Grace

Further, he writes: 'To keep me from being too elated by the abundance of revelations, a thorn was given me in the flesh, a messenger of Satan, to harass me, to keep me from being too elated. Three times I besought the Lord about this, that it should leave me; but He said to me, "My grace is sufficient for you, for my power is made perfect in weakness."' (2 Cor. 12, 7-9)

St Paul describes his condition candidly. He does not say he is sick but that a spike was put into his flesh, a thorn that remained there. The thorn left him no peace. Paul had to bear the piercing, jabbing pain. It never left him and cost him sleepless nights. Pain was his closest companion.

To the present day, nobody knows exactly what is meant by this 'spike'. Is it physical pain, e.g. stomach pain, heart trouble ... or mental suffering such as fear or sadness, or even something like epilepsy, giving him fits? There are some indications of this. We know nothing with certainty and can only guess what it might have been. In any case, this thorn driven into his flesh, as he says figuratively, must have been very severe and painful at times and a hindrance to his work. Paul had a hard time. The constant pain prevented him from achieving a great deal as he had wanted to.

There are very many people today suffering in body or soul. The one has been plagued by physical suffering for years; another is suffering mentally and yet another suffers both ways. Nearly everyone has a burden to carry. St Paul says he entreated the Lord three times, praying to be freed from this pressure of suffering, this piercing pain, these infernal, mean blows from God's opponent. God, however, did not allow him to have what he asked for. God did not grant his request. The spike was not removed.

It was the same with Jesus. He implored the Father three times: 'Let this cup pass by me...!' But the cup did not pass by. Why? This will always be a secret. Apparently God had another plan. Instead, an angel came to Jesus to strengthen Him.

Are not all the things we ask for in our prayers granted to us, prayers we send up to Heaven in critical situations? This question is certainly a problem, since God Himself invites us to call upon Him and even literally pester Him; He never leaves us empty-handed. The answer to this pressing question must be, with regard to St Paul: God always hears and answers us but differently, more mysteriously, more wondrously than we sometimes can imagine. Paul is the star witness of how God answers us: He might not always do what I so dearly want. However, He does give my heart incredible strength, which makes me, temporarily or permanently a weak person, strong to an incredible degree.

God has only agreed to give us His grace and to be near us and not abandon us. This is sufficient. This consoles us. Still, some answers may be obtained: 'My grace is sufficient for you!' Do not worry! Each day you are given so much strength, the right amount, enough for you to endure the thorn. You are not to think to yourself that you must bear this burden all your life. A wise person divides his life up into hours and the hours into minutes; now is when I must endure!

'Grace attains perfection in weakness!' God uses the weakness of people to reveal His omnipotence: 'When I am weak, I am strong!' (2 Cor. 12, 13)

Consider the priest of Ars in France. His Church superiors said he was too stupid to become a priest. It was only because a priest vouched for him and was willing to take him as a chaplain that he was finally ordained. For a long time he was not allowed to hear Confession. In the end he was sent to a parish where they thought he could really make no mistakes. Then he made the whole world listen! Each one of the thousands of people who came to confess was a drop in the ocean that corrected the thinking of those in charge.

We should not forget something very important concerning suffering. St Paul thinks his suffering is totally necessary because, through this suffering, he can 'supplement the sufferings of Christ'! Paul knows that 'God is loyal; He will not allow you to be tempted beyond your strength. He will create a way out of temptation for you, so that you can succeed.' There is what we might call 'spiritual barter' within the body of Christ. If a paraplegic somewhere bears his suffering patiently, it can take effect in, say, Central Africa, India, Japan or Canada. We will get a surprise when the curtain is finally drawn aside and the cards are laid face-up on the table. (Cf. 1 Peter 3ff.) The one with the thorn cannot cope all alone. Valiant 'helpers in the faith' are needed.

The courage of the faith involved here is not to be under-estimated. A person who wants to learn swimming cannot stay standing on the shore. He has to get into the water and entrust himself to this element. It is relatively easy when the swimming teacher is within reach. Similarly, each of us has to entrust himself to the element of grace. Christ is always at hand.

(Cf. Anton Kner PuK No. 4, 1982, 439-441)

God hears what we pray for with our heart:

Branimir is a Christian and a great believer. Everyone notices this. When he talks with people, he succeeds in drawing their attention to what is essential and most important in life. Once, when he was travelling and he put up at a hotel, there was a girl working as a waitress, whom he asked if she had time to pray every day. She answered, "We have so much work to do here, you know, that we scarcely get time to eat anything. How are we supposed to find time to pray too?"

"Let me teach you a short prayer," he said, "consisting of only three words: 'Jesus, save me!' It is in the Holy Scriptures, in Matthew 14, 30. Try to pray this once in the morning and once in the evening!" The girl promised she would.

After some months, our friend returned to this hotel. He learned that the girl had left, was given her address and decided to call on her. "Oh, my friend," said the girl spontaneously, having recognized him immediately, "do you know what your prayer did for me? I prayed it every morning and every evening for 15 days, as I promised you. After that I started to wonder what this prayer might mean. You told me it is in the Bible, so I got myself one. Through reading it I learned two things: first of all, that

I must be saved and, secondly, that Jesus has saved me! I cannot say the prayer any more now, for it has been heard. Every day and every moment I say, 'Thank you, Lord, for hearing my prayer!' I also give my thanks to God for sending you to me!"

Do we take time to pray and to read the Word of God? Perhaps we do not feel it is necessary, because we dc not feel guilty of anything. If this is the case, it is vital to ask God to show us our sins clearly. He will certainly do so and we shall definitely be able to experience the same thing as this girl. This example shows us convincingly what Our Lady constantly teaches us, namely that God hears any prayer if we just pray it with love in our heart.

the visionary Mirjana

Pray the Rosary Every Day!

The Rosary is a powerful, wonderful and perfect prayer! It is exalted, beautiful and ingenious! It is a prayer for everybody, any time and anywhere!

Once there was an old lady sitting in the tram with two little children on her lap, both of them wearing a mourning crape. They were apparently her grandchildren or orphans. She had a rosary in her hand. An old man was sitting opposite her. It was clear that the two children had lost a parent and that they must have been a burden to their grandmother.

The old man said, "You seem to have a lot of worries."

"I am filled with hope and consolation!"

"How can that be?"

"Because of this." She showed him the rosary. "I pray the joyful mysteries for these orphans, for Our Lady to cheer them. I pray the glorious mysteries for my dead son and the sorrowful mysteries for myself," she said with tears in her eyes, "so that God may protect me and I can look after these children well and lose neither my strength nor my patience."

There are only two types of Christians: those who pray and those who do not pray. This was said by a saint. Perhaps we can add something and say that there are two types of Christians: those who pray the Rosary and those who do not pray it. That is, however, surely not expressed right. There is only one type of believing Christian.

Those who never pray to God will have difficulty in remaining true Christians. Our faith is belief that includes prayer and the worship of God. Whoever does not pray does not deserve the name 'Christian'.

When we pray the Rosary, it is important, even essential, to reflect, together with the Blessed Virgin Mary, on the life, death and resurrection of our Saviour and thereby to worship God with one's thoughts and call on Him for help. This way we can, through Mary's example, share in the life, pain and glory of the Lord. This is the essential part of any true and profound prayer. Therefore we can say rightly that the Rosary is a prayer in keeping with Jesus' instructions, with St Paul's preaching and with the way our Church has always prayed.

The Prayer of the Rosary is a continual, lasting and devoted prayer, which gives praise and thanks to our God, because He created us and we receive from Him everything we need. In God's name we pray the Rosary, with our attention focused on what we pray; we thank God 50 times for Christ's love and His taking on flesh to become a person, 50 times for the love which Jesus showed us through His suffering and His death, 50 times for the love which awaits us in Heaven when we are resurrected and 150 times for the love of His Holy Mother Mary. One can rightly say the Rosary is a summary of the Gospel, with the exception of the last two glorious mysteries, these two being based exclusively on the teachings of the Holy Roman Catholic Church.

Whenever we pray the joyful mysteries of the Rosary, we think of Jesus and Mary and how she conceived Him through the Holy Spirit, took Him to visit Elizabeth, gave birth to Him in the stable in Bethlehem, offered Him up in the temple and found Him there again after searching for Him for three days.

Whenever we pray the sorrowful mysteries, we contemplate the torments of Jesus before He walked to Calvary, when we accompany Him and help Him to carry the heavy cross, just as Simon of Cyrene did. Similarly to His favourite disciple John, we stand under the cross with Mary.

Finally, when we pray the glorious mysteries of the Rosary, we unite in the Holy Spirit with Jesus, who was resurrected and went up to heavenly Paradise and also with the apostles, whom Jesus promised the gift of the Holy Spirit; He sent them this Spirit soon afterwards. We think of the heavenly splendour in which Mary, the saints and all the chosen ones live.

In the Rosary, we thus contemplate the whole of the salvation, the whole life of Jesus and all His works and deeds. We pray fervently with the words of the Lord's Prayer; with the Hail Mary, the prayer which, through the Gospel of St Luke, is attributed partly to Holy Archangel Gabriel and partly to St Elizabeth, the mother of St John the Baptist; with the Glory Be to the Father, the prayer of St Paul; and with the Creed, the prayer of all Christians.

The Lord's Prayer contains the most beautiful words of the Son of God. The Hail Mary contains the most beautiful words of an angel and a saint on earth. The Glory Be to the Father is wonderfully exalted. The Creed is the expression of the whole wisdom of our faith and everything positive about life!

The Rosary is therefore a perfect prayer in itself. It satisfies all our needs and so places the whole person with body and soul in the service of God.

This is the Time of Grace

Numerous Popes, especially in the last one hundred years recommend and give their preference to the Prayer of the Rosary, to the point where we cannot ignore this.

Pope Pius XI said, "Through the Rosary we will convert the opponents of religion and will ourselves attain a life of virtue in accordance with the Gospel."

Pope Pius XII, at the request of Our Lady of Fatima, consecrated the whole world to the Immaculate Heart of Mary in 1942 and began his prayer of consecration with the words: "Queen of the Rosary, refuge of humanity, victor in all of God's battles ..."

Pope John XXIII prayed the Rosary enthusiastically and he never omitted it.

Pope Paul VI said that the Prayer of the Rosary is the best weapon for achieving peace.

Pope John Paul II prayed the Rosary every day, despite his more than heavy work load and, on his numerous journeys, he consecrated the peoples of the earth to the heart of Mary, the heart of our Mother.

Certainly one can live as a Catholic without the Rosary but the fact that the Church trusts and loves this prayer so much is something that sets one thinking. The reason is that this prayer contains everything that is relevant to our life. In the Rosary, we contemplate fifteen secrets of our Saviour and, at the same time, the same number of mysteries of the souls He has saved.

This is because the mysteries of His childhood and His birth are also the mysteries of our being children of God and our rebirth. The mysteries of His suffering and death are the mysteries of our suffering, dying and our being crucified with the Lord. The mysteries of His being resurrected and glorified are the promises of our resurrection, our victory and our living in blessedness with the Father.

With what joy, gratitude and love we can therefore contemplate the five joyful mysteries of the Rosary! As Mary conceived the Son of God, so we were allowed to receive Him too when we became children of God. As Mary took Him to Elizabeth, we are allowed to have Him with us in our hearts and take Him to the people we visit. As Mary gave birth to the Son of God for the world, so too should we tell others of Christ and give Him to them. As Mary made her offering of the godly child in the temple and of herself too, we are allowed to offer Him in every Holy Mass and offer ourselves too. As Mary, filled with pain, looked for the lost child, our life is a search for God, often a painful one, until we find Him. In all these mysteries of the childhood of Jesus, the Immaculate Heart of Mary shines in humility, love, faithfulness and devotion.

The Rosary is the prayer of our life; to what extent is shown by the five sorrowful mysteries of the sufferings of Jesus. Each mystery is a source of strength for our life and sufferings, for the Son of God has already borne all our sufferings with love. With Him we are able to bear our fears, our fear of pain and illness, our fear of separation and death. With Him we are able to bear the blows of the scourge we suffer in our life, the blows of lovelessness, the blows of injustice. With Him we are able to wear the crown of thorns, the thorns of being scorned, the thorns of slander. With Him we are able, especially, to bear our cross, the cross of carrying out our duty conscientiously, the cross of illness, the cross of getting old. With Him we are able to die worthily. No-one who entrusts himself to the arms of Jesus dies alone!

68   This is the Time of Grace

Next comes the wonderful vision of the reality of the future. In the five glorious mysteries of the Rosary, this prayer enters the dimension of eternity. Here we can contemplate the fulfilment of our own lives. With the Son of God, to whom we belong inseparably, we will be resurrected! With Him we will live in Heaven at the right hand of the Father in joy so great that it is indescribable! Through the coming of the Spirit, we will be allowed to be part of the new Heaven and live on the new earth, where God is everything. There we will be allowed to live in peace and unimaginable bliss; with body and soul in fulfilment that Our Lady has already attained through her assumption and coronation in Heaven.

This is why the Rosary is the prayer of our life. There is surely no prayer better suited to expressing our love for God, our gratitude for our salvation and our belief in eternal splendour than the Prayer of the Rosary and the contemplation of its mysteries.

Time spent in prayer is the time we use best. All our petitions and our problems, whether personal ones or the wider ones of the Church and the world, do not get solved through talking at length; rather, they are best solved through prayer.

Artists of significance who prayed the Rosary every day:

Beethoven, a great musical genius, loved to pray the Rosary every day.

Michelangelo, a great artistic genius, prayed the Rosary and took on the challenge of painting the Sistine Chapel; here he depicted, et al., the Blessed Virgin Mary taking souls out of purgatory with the rosary. His rosary has been kept in Florence to the present day.

Gluck, the musician, was found, when he died, with his hand clasping a rosary.

Ampere, a scientific genius of recent times, prayed the Rosary in church every day.

Ozanam, who was famous, was converted when he saw how Ampere prayed the Rosary in church.

Recamier, a great medical doctor, one day left his rosary on the operating table. His colleagues were atheists and were speechless with amazement. When would the best French doctor be praying the Rosary? The doctor said, "Yes, gentlemen, I pray the Rosary. When I have no hope for a patient and when medicine cannot help, I reach for the rosary and, believe me, with it I am enviably successful!"

The conversion of a Viennese schoolboy:

The lad had just completed seventh class and was an unbeliever but, since his father wished him to, he still went to scripture lessons. Then came the day of the Corpus Christi procession. He promised his father that he would be there too. He was among the spectators and was making jokes about those who went in the procession, until... a group of Catholic railwaymen came past. His father was among them, with his head down and praying the Rosary.

"I have always loved my father and seen him as the person I value most. I had never liked him more than at that moment. I did not know a person could be as lovely as my father is when he is praying the Rosary! Since then I have been a practising Catholic. I would like to become similar to my father."

This is the Time of Grace

The tireless appeal of the Queen of Peace to pray the Rosary every day:

Our Lady said in a message on 14 August, 1984: "I would like the people to pray with me in these present days, as many of you as possible; and to fast strictly on Wednesdays and Fridays; and to pray at least the Rosary every day, the joyful, sorrowful and glorious mysteries."

On 25 January, 1991, she said: "Dear children! Today, as never before, I invite you to prayer. Let your prayer be a prayer for peace. Satan is strong and desires to destroy not only human life, but also nature and the planet on which you live. Therefore, dear children, pray that through prayer you can protect yourselves with God's blessing of peace. God has sent me among you so that I may help you. If you so wish, grasp for the rosary. Even the rosary alone can work miracles in the world and in your lives. I bless you and I remain with you for as long as it is God's will. Thank you for not betraying my presence here and I thank you because your response is serving the good and the peace."

Our Lady has said that we can defeat Satan with the rosary in our hand. (8 August, 1985)

A man in despair implored a priest to save his soul:

One evening the doorbell of the parsonage rang. The priest opened the window and asked who it was and what he wanted. A middle-aged man simply called out, "Father, save my soul!" The priest opened the door and spoke to him. The man looked like a beggar.

He said to the priest, "Listen to me for a moment. I used not to be like this. I was like any other youth but also very much a believer and very pious. I have my mother to thank for that; she brought me up to be like that. She always entreated me to be good. I promised her again and again that I would be but I kept breaking my promise.

'I began to drink and lost my job. I became lazy and a thief. Earlier today I was waiting for a man who was coming home from work. I knew he had got paid today. I jumped him and took his wallet with the money in it.

'Suddenly I saw a rosary in his hand and got such a fright that I gave him back his money and asked him to give me the rosary. The poor man was absolutely astounded. I went a bit farther away, sat on a wall and then looked at the rosary. Then something strange happened: I had a vision of my mother praying the Rosary. I heard her say, "My son, I am always praying the Rosary for you; please be converted!" So you see, that is why I came here at once. Help me and save my soul! My mother said I could make a confession immediately."

The priest heard his confession straight away and, from that moment, the despairing man began to lead a new life.

The Rosary is powerful and wondrous. It has restored many people to life and has been their prayer of salvation.

This is the Time of Grace

Go to Confession each Month!

The Sacrament of reconciliation, Confession, is the one in which God forgives us all our sins if we just repent of them sincerely and decide, with God's help, to want not to sin again. This is the sacrament that is rich in grace and heals us. Confession is a spiritual resurrection. It is the joyous encounter of a small, sinful person with his great, merciful brother, Jesus Christ, who is present in His Church.

A Christian goes to Confession because he is aware that, in the view of the faith, he did not treat other people as brothers and did not love God as the Father. Aware that he has transgressed against the duty to be loving, he goes to Confession because his mistake pains him and he seeks to restore his friendship with God in Christ through the grace of reconciliation and absolution.

Through this Sacrament of atonement, a Christian receives back the holiness of his Baptism in a special way, sin having damaged it to a greater or lesser extent. When an adult Christian is saved, he is saved through Confession. When he loses the purity of his soul, he loses it through not going regularly to Confession.

Confession is a great grace which God grants; it is the valuable Easter gift for His followers from Christ resurrected. God keeps inviting us to come back to Him, whenever we decide to return to Him and repent of our own sins. He is glad to forgive us and in so doing He guides us to our eternal joy.

"We are all sinners; we are all wounded through sin. The wounded, however, need medicines and healing. That is just what Confession is. It is healing and restoration to health. It heals our wounded heart. It makes a sick soul healthy. The doctor and healer is always the Lord God, none other; the mediator in this case is the priest, the confessor ..." (Jacob Bubalo)

Confession was given us by our Saviour as the prerequisite for reconciliation. It is a beautiful reflection of God's goodness, which is always prepared to forgive. Let us not forget: sin is everything that we do, say, think and want but that is not pleasing to God.

The most serious sin, also called a mortal sin, is spiritual suicide in the truest sense. It takes our life of grace from us, without which there is no blessedness in eternity. We have killed ourselves as often as we have committed a serious sin. Confession gives us back the life we lost. After that, our spiritual powers develop. In such cases, Confession always means resurrection.

How can one make a good confession?

Confession is, in a way, accusing oneself. Those who are not used to it are scared, not of confessing but of the priest; so they are worried about the unnecessary and unbearable question of what he will say about it. This question, however, should not concern us. We must consciously, voluntarily, repentantly and totally present ourselves before God and His representative. This is the first condition for reconciliation.

What do we need, to do this? We need the awareness that we have erred and thereby have sinned against God and our neighbour. It is necessary to check our own thoughts, words, deeds and shortcomings and admit them sincerely and openly to our own conscience and then to God's agent, the priest. Our own awareness should accuse our own conscience courageously, uncompromisingly, convincingly, without omissions and
74

without indulgence. This is the first condition for a good, valid confession.

Our godly Saviour introduced Holy Confession as a condition for obtaining forgiveness. God is prepared to forgive us for everything and for every way in which we have sinned: in deeds, thoughts, words and wishes.

The following are necessarily present in a good confession: awareness, willingness, humility, completeness, repentance and the courage to confess all our sins to God and His representative. Confession assumes repentance and the firm resolution not to sin any more.

What does 'repent' mean? To 'repent' means to regret deep down that we have offended God and a fellow-human being. There are two sorts of repentance: complete repentance and incomplete repentance, depending on the reason for which we feel repentance. There is complete repentance when we regret that we have offended the unlimited goodness of the Father and so were unfaithful to the love with which we are loved. Repentance of this kind enables us to be forgiven our sins immediately. That is why it is complete or perfect repentance. Incomplete repentance is the one we feel when we repent of our sins through fear of God's punishment or fear of hell. It is also good and suffices for Confession. If love cannot save somebody, fear can, fear being the beginning of wisdom. Repentance, i.e. sincere and deep regret, is essential to a good confession; without it, a confession cannot be a good one. The awareness that we have trespassed can prompt deep regret in our heart.

True repentance is unthinkable without the wish and the firm resolve to cease to commit a sin. This decision is the main part of repentance, a necessary effect. The break with sin must be radical in our wishes, our intentions and our decisions. Many people do not understand this and say they are sure they will sin again. They know themselves. They have often promised to stop committing a sin and then sinned again.

To avoid any misunderstanding: we are not required never to fall. It is expected and required of us that we fight against sin. We should avoid every circumstance that leads us to sin. This determination must be clear in a confession. The priest must and should be able to recognize this determination. That is sufficient for a confession to be valid. God then gives us as much strength as we need for the fight against sin. When we confessed and our confession was valid, we made the right decision, which means we confessed well.

There are those who say, "I am not going to Confession because I do not want to cheat. I promised something and yet I fell into sin again." This assumption is wrong! Whoever repents sincerely does not cheat anybody! Falling is the result of our weakness and our innate imperfection. The purpose of Confession is to strengthen us spiritually. The only person who cheats is the one who does not sincerely repent. Whoever sincerely repents deserves forgiveness; we can be sure of that.

It can, unfortunately, happen that, at Confession, someone fails to mention or denies a serious sin, out of fear and shame. Whoever denies a serious sin at Confession cannot be forgiven a single sin by God. One cannot deceive God! He knows everything!

Such a confession would be really fateful. The saving of our soul for eternity is at stake: happiness or perdition. We cannot treat our soul as a joke! It is better not to go to Confession than not to experience conversion at Confession.

76

Any confession that was not good and any sacrilege at Holy Communion can be 'corrected' through a new, honest confession. We must just find a priest as quickly as possible, whom we can tell everything, including the fact that we did not make a good confession before. Any priest will be pleased and Jesus will be especially pleased that one is again in a state of grace.

To be able to make a good confession, it is important to ask the Holy Spirit for enlightenment. That is why we must examine our conscience. We must mend our ways, repent and decide not to sin any more. It is necessary really to tell the priest everything and to do the penance given us.

We can examine our conscience as follows:

Am I at peace with everyone? Am I at enmity with anyone? If so, why?

Do I forgive everyone as God forgives me?

Who is God to me? Do I really believe in God or am I a prey to doubt, disbelief, loss of faith, mistrust of God, idolatry, dabbling in the occult and magic; do I tend to utter curses, whether serious ones or those we are tempted to deny as being curses?

Do I love God above all else and my neighbour as myself?

Do I work hard on Sundays and holidays?

Do I fail to attend Holy Mass on Sundays and to pray every day?

Do I lack concentration during prayers?

Do I go to Confession at least twice a year and receive Holy Communion?

Do I read the Holy Scriptures (possibly also Church newspapers) and do I try to find out more about the teaching of the Church?

Do I honour my parents and old people?

Do I have my children brought up and educated according to the Church? Have I hit anyone?

Have I killed anyone?

Have I criticized anyone unfairly?

Have I slandered anyone?

Have I cursed anyone?

Have I stolen? Have I lied? Have I borne false witness?

Have I drunk too much? Have I smoked immoderately?

Have I damaged my health?

Have I done anything unchaste? Have I thought, wished, expressed or observed anything impure? Did I have or am I having a relationship before marriage?

Have I committed adultery? Have I masturbated?

Have I read pornographic magazines or books? Have I watched pornographic films or listened to pornographic tapes?

Am I arrogant, vain, greedy, jealous, selfish, envious or malicious?

Am I lazy or irresponsible at work?

This is the Time of Grace

Do I get annoyed about the mistakes of others?

Do I let trivial things annoy me?

What is my worst fault? Do I strive to overcome it?

Do I purify my thoughts and ideas?

Prayer of Contrition:

I sincerely repent of all my sins, because through them I have deeply offended God, the one I value most; He is the greatest and dearest Father. I wish to try very hard to keep my good resolution and to become a better person. Jesus, forgive me and help me. Amen.

Father Petar celebrating Holy Mass in Medjugorje

Conscience Check according to the Ten Commandments

I AM THE LORD, YOUR GOD!	DO THE FOLLOWING! BE VIRTUOUS!	AVOID THE FOLLO-WING!
1. **You shall have no other gods besides Me!**	Honour and aknow-ledge God through belief, hope and love! Pray! Honour Our Lady, the angels and the saints!	disregard for belief, hope und love; sacrilege, superstition, fail-ure to pray
2. **You shall not take the name of the Lord, your God, in vain!**	Honour the name of God and the names of the saints! One may only swear an oath when necessary and one may not break it!	misuse of the name of God; curses , blasphemies, condemning, perjury
3. **Remember to keep the Lord's day holy!**	Observe Sunday as holy and avoid hard work on Sun-days! Go to Holy Mass!	working hard on a Sunday; missing Holy Mass voluntarily (serious sin!)
4. **You shall hon-our your fa-ther and mother!**	Honour and love your parents and obey them!	failure to obey and respect one's parent(s)
5. **You shall not kill!**	Live sensibly and moderately! Take care of your health and your life and that of your neighbour!	harming the life or well-being of one-self or another; getting angry, drinking to excess, killing an unborn child, hating, (etc.)

This is the Time of Grace

6.	You shall not commit adultery!	Be chaste and pure! This applies to thoughts, words and deeds! Before marriage and outside marriage, sexual relations are prohibited!	indecency (impure thoughts, words or deeds); indecent books or pictures, masturbation, sins with others (serious sins!)
7.	You shall not steal!	Observe justice! Give everyone what belongs to him! Respect the property of others! Make amends for any wrongs!	theft, deception, exploitation, harming another person
8.	You shall not give false witness against your neighbour!	Love the truth! Say only what you really think! Keep your word! Be discreet!	lying, wicked gossip, slander
9.	You shall not covet your neighbour's wife!	In marriage stay faithful and love one another until death!	adultery (sin with another partner) (whether in deeds or thoughts)
10.	You shall not covet your neighbour's property!	Restrain yourself and avoid greed!	coveting what belongs to someone else

Conscience Check according to the Church's Commandments

COMMANDMENT	DO THE FOLLOWING! BE VIRTUOUS!	AVOID THE FOLLOWING!
1. Observe the official Church holidays; go to Holy Mass on those days and Sundays; be reverent at Holy Mass!	Church holidays: Christmas (25 Dec.) Ascension Whitsuntide/Pentecost Corpus Christi (ten days after Pentecost) Assumption (15 Aug.) All Saints' (1 Nov.) Easter (most important!)	missing Holy Mass voluntarily (serious sin!) working hard on Sundays and Church holidays (if for several hours, a serious sin!)
2. Fast on the official fasting days; do not eat meat on certain days!	Fasting : fasting is obligatory on Ash Wednesday and Good Friday from 21 to 60 years of age; one meal (at most) but little else is allowed. Forgoing of meat: eating meat is forbidden on Fridays during Lent and on Ash Wednesday; this is obligatory from the age of 14 years for the rest of one's life.	failure to fast and to forgo meat (if frequent and unjustified, a serious sin!) The following people are excused from forgoing meat: those eating in a refectory, for instance; sick people; convalescents; those doing strenuous work, etc. One is no longer obliged to forgo meat on Fridays other than Fridays in Lent; however doing good deeds is recommended, e.g. reading from the Holy Bible, abstaining from alcohol and cigarettes, helping someone.

This is the Time of Grace

3.	Go to Confession and Communion at least once a year (preferably at Easter)!	Yearly Confession and Communion: this is a minimum; the latter should be received during the 50 days of Easter (Easter to Pentecost) if possible. If you cannot go to church, ask a priest to visit you at home.	omission of yearly Confession and Holy Communion (possibly a serious sin!)
4.	Observe the laws of matrimony of the Holy Church!	A Church wedding: this is the beginning of a Christian marriage. Respect and value the goals of marriage, attend to the children's upbringing and help the spouse entrusted to you.	non-observance of the sacrament of marriage, including, within marriage: forbidden avoidance of having children (e.g. through contraception); bringing up children badly; neglecting one's spouse (serious sin!)
5.	Make a contribution towards meeting the needs of the Church!	The needs of the Church: the faithful have a duty to help the Church to function (in training priests, in the mission, in the church, etc.).	refusal to do one's duty towards the Church when one could do it

Holy Mass should be your Life!

What is Holy Mass (the Eucharist)?

The Eucharist is the mystery of all mysteries. A true and proper Christian sees this mystery as the source of belief and life. It is the heart and soul of our faith. It is the focus and the zenith of Christianity.

St Augustine says: "I dare to assert that God could not give us more, even though He is almighty, and that He did not know what more there was to give, even though He is infinitely rich, when He left us Holy Mass."

We are told that Holy Mass is the bloodless sacrifice of the new Covenant, in which Jesus Christ offers Himself perpetually to His heavenly Father in the form of bread and wine. We should firmly believe, above all, that Holy Mass is a true and present reality; a present event and our joyous encounter with the resurrected Christ, who makes His holy sacrifice present for us, here and now. In every Holy Mass, Christ sacrifices Himself for us and shows us His love. It is this same love that led Him to embrace the cross, to carry it to Calvary, to die in great pain on the cross, to be laid in the grave and to rise again on the third day.

To be present at Holy Mass means consciously accepting the encounter with the living Christ and even meeting God through Christ, according to His own words; meeting Him who loves us endlessly and gives Himself to us at Holy Communion. To be present at Holy Mass also means being together with our brothers and sisters in Christ and with the whole Church. It means, first, being present through one's own decision and, secondly, having resolved to give Him love, friendship and faithfulness

84

and, thirdly, offering oneself, so that one is richer in grace and in all other virtues.

Our High Priest, Jesus Christ, sacrificed His life to His heavenly Father once and for all on the cross. Immediately before His sacrifice, Christ held the Last Supper with His disciples. He gave them the portions of bread and the chalice of wine and said: 'This is my body .... This is my blood ....' That was the first Holy Mass.

Christ's suffering, death and resurrection is the genuine salvation of the whole of humanity; the past, the present and the future are all included. The sacrifice of the Mass on our altars is the commemoration of the Last Supper and the sacrifice on the cross. It is not an empty remembrance and not the revival of a memory of an event. It is the present reality of the event of salvation, renewed again and again, in which the Church offers to the Heavenly Father the sacrifice of His Son. Thus, this unique sacrifice is made reality for us through the liturgical and sacramental renewal; it becomes our sacrifice, 'here and now', Jesus Christ, who once and for all made His true sacrifice of salvation. It is indeed a true sacrifice, as is His death on the cross.

Therefore the daily celebration of Holy Mass is not a repetition of the sacrifice of Christ but its present realization. It remains the one and only sacrifice. It is the true presence now; it is an eternal Last Supper; such is this celebration of Holy Communion using bread and wine. Holy Mass is Easter, for the resurrected Jesus Christ is present. It is also Mount Calvary, for it grants us a share in the gifts of the Passion and makes the sacrifice eternal that was begun there.

Holy Mass is the greatest gift that Christ gave to humanity. It is the most valuable thing we Catholic Christians possess. Holy Mass is a great stream of grace, which gushes forth from beneath the cross. It washes the sinful earth clean, purifies our soul and makes it holy, heals it and saves it.

At Holy Mass, a sinner becomes a saint, a child of human parents becomes a child of God and a condemned person becomes a blessed person. Out of darkness one goes into holiness. At Holy Mass we also serve our God, for we devote ourselves to Him with our faith and our trust, so that He can teach us. All the graces for the Christians and the Church are derived from Holy Mass.

How should we experience Holy Mass?

It is very important, above all, for us to experience Holy Mass with our whole being, that is, with body and soul, filled with belief, hope and love, actively and consciously, humbly, devoutly and devotedly.

Let us take ourselves and our whole life to the celebration of Holy Mass. We should not forget to place all our sinfulness on the altar with the water in the chalice, so that He cleanses us of it, similarly all our sacrifices, sufferings, problems, wishes and prayers, so that Jesus takes everything and makes it holy, makes new people of us, absolves us and saves us .

At Holy Mass, Jesus gives us the opportunity to encounter Him personally. We encounter Him not only in the spiritual sense but also visibly. Always when we receive His body and His blood, we encounter Him, for Christ is truly present in the form of   bread and wine. This is not only a mystery but also true reality for us.

This is the Time of Grace

The Queen of Peace wishes Holy Mass to become our life:

No-one can tell us better than Our Lady, the Mother of Jesus, what great, eternal gift of God to us Holy Mass is! She teaches us how to experience and live this most joyous encounter with God. She knows best what it means to us to be with Jesus and to live with the eucharistic Jesus in a truly eucharistic way. She would like Holy Mass to be our life and our life to be Holy Mass. Only then does life acquire its full meaning and then we know why we exist and that it is worth being alive.

The Blessed Virgin Mary says in her message of 3.4.1986: "Dear children! I wish to call you to a living of the Holy Mass. There are many of you who have sensed the beauty of the Holy Mass, but there are also those who come unwillingly. I have chosen you, dear children, but Jesus gives you His graces in the Mass. Therefore, consciously live the Holy Mass and let your coming to it be a joyful one. Come to it with love and make the Mass your own."

Holy Mass should be an encounter that is most joyous, happy, blessed and beneficial to us. A great many pilgrims, who have visited Medjugorje, the shrine of the Queen of Peace, have discovered the immeasurable value of Holy Mass. "That was the most beautiful Mass of my life!" A girl from Germany said this, adding: "I shall never forget the pilgrims' evening Mass. The joy I felt during Mass was so indescribable that it keeps drawing me back to Medjugorje."

The message of 25.4.1988 says that Holy Mass is the focal point of life; it is even life itself; a church is the palace of God, consecrated to the presence of God; we are all invited to holiness, which comes from our encounter with the Holy One.

"Dear children! God wants to make you holy. Therefore, through me He is inviting you to complete surrender. Let Holy Mass be your life. Understand that the church is God's palace, the place in which I gather you and want to show you the way to God. Come and pray. Neither look at others nor slander them, but rather, let your life be a testimony on the way of holiness. Churches deserve respect and are set apart as holy because God, who became man, dwells in them day and night. Therefore, little children, believe and pray that the Father increase your faith, and then ask for whatever you need. I am with you and I am rejoicing because of your conversion and I am protecting you with my motherly mantle..."

To be a good, conscientious Christian, honest and holy, is the duty of each and every person, especially a Catholic. Holiness is a gift of grace that only God can give. One is holy if one tries to fulfil the will of God every moment of one's life; one whose thoughts, words and actions, indeed whose whole life is in keeping with God's will.

Whoever, therefore, has great and perfect trust in God, whoever believes in God at every moment, whoever says to God, "Here I am, Lord, for Your will to be done concerning me and everybody, now and always!" is a person on the sure path to holiness. Holy Mass, as the greatest and most perfect prayer, makes us holiest and makes us into new people of God.

"Dear children! I want to tell you that this season is especially for you from the parish. When it is summer, you see that you have a lot of work. Now you don't have work in the fields, work on your own self personally! Come to Mass because this is the season given to you. Dear children, there are enough of those who come regularly despite bad weather because they love me and wish to show their love in a special way. What I want from you is to show me your love by coming to Mass, and the Lord will reward you abundantly." (21.11.1985)

Our Lady would especially like to point out to us that the time at our disposal is a gift of God. We are not to play with this time. We must use it better to work on ourselves and we must recognize its value. How a person spends his time determines what person he will be. The best thing is to devote our time to God and spend it where we, as people, can employ it most valuably and most worthily, consecrate it and use it to the greatest advantage.

We spend most of our time with what we like and with what makes us happy. When we do something for God, when we give God first place in our lives, we will spend our most valuable time with God, at the sacrifice of Holy Mass. That way we dedicate our time and ourselves too. Then we grow to be people of God, apostles of brotherly love and peace. This is the reward Our Lady speaks of. Of course, God prepares a big surprise for us in Heaven, for every minute we spent lovingly in company with Him.

"Dear children! I am calling you to more active prayer and attendance at Holy Mass. I wish your Mass to be an experience of God. I wish especially to say to the young people: be open to the Holy Spirit because God wishes to draw you to Himself in these days when Satan is at work…" (16.5.1985)

Nowhere can we feel and experience the proximity of God as at the sacrifice of Holy Mass. We are told that Jesus is with us during Holy Mass and Jesus is in us during Holy Communion. We receive the living God in our heart and thus unite with Him. In order to be able to experience God, it is necessary to be totally open to Him, to devote oneself to Him, to repent of all one's sins and to allow Him to surround us, bless us, guide us and sanctify us with His Spirit.

Our Lady came to be with us, to strengthen us in withstanding our temptations. That is why she repeatedly renews her call to conversion, atonement, strong faith, renewal of family prayer and attending Holy Mass:

"Dear children! Today I call you to renew prayer in your families. Dear children, encourage the very young to prayer and the children to go to Holy Mass. Thank you for having responded to my call." (7.3.1985)

We are all invited to be present but the children are especially, so that they come to know, as early as possible, what the heart and soul of our faith is: Holy Mass. It is our holy duty to guide them and give them a good example. The best example is to participate joyfully in this high celebration.

A family who discovered the value of Holy Mass:

The family had been to Lourdes and Fatima a few times. They had come to Medjugorje and grown fond of it because here their faith had become alive and they had come to know the value of prayer, especially the value of Holy Mass. Several times a year they came to Medjugorje. Their son was addicted to alcohol and during Holy Mass they always prayed for him, "Lord, You can do all things; please hear the Queen of Peace as she mediates for us; please help our son! Convert him and free him from all dependencies! We give everything to You and consecrate everything to You! May Your will be done concerning him!"

This is the Time of Grace

His parents prayed some Rosaries for him every day, went to Holy Mass every day to thank God and God heard their prayer. Their son came to Medjugorje after a very serious car accident that had nearly cost him his life. Here he experienced his own encounter with Jesus. He was converted to the point of making his life's confession and then began to pray more and more every day. His heart became so open to God and the influence of the Holy Spirit was so strong that he has since answered God's call. He began studying theology, became a deacon and is soon to be ordained as a priest.

Seeing that God had heard their prayer, his parents now fasted for the conversion of their daughter. Again God heard their prayer. She was converted and now prays a great deal. She is now so close to God that she makes a pilgrimage each month to a well-known place of pilgrimage of Our Lady. God can really do all things when we seek His will in everything and do everything for His honour.

> "Our entire person shall tremble,
> the whole world shall shake
> and Heaven shall rejoice
> when on the altar in the priest's hands
> Christ is present,
> the Son of the living God!"
> (Francis of Assisi)

Read and Live the Holy Bible!

A man named Miroslav went up to Father Emanuel and told him briefly that he wanted a Baptism. When the priest asked him why he had thought of it and decided for it at this point in his life, the man answered, "I have read the Bible and I have come to know Jesus Christ, who is the Saviour of all of us. He clearly says you cannot be saved if you have not been baptised."

The priest was not sure at first whether to take him seriously and asked him, "Where did you get the Bible in a country such as this?"

"I am an employer, you see, and I was just going to inspect some of the buildings by the railway line. A train was going past and I saw someone throw something out of the moving train. It landed right in front of my feet. It was a Bible."

"Do you have that Bible with you?" asked the priest.

The man answered in the affirmative. When the priest took the book in his hands, he immediately recognized it as his own Bible. All this took place some years ago in Georgia in the former U.S.S.R. Today there is freedom of worship there. What had happened, though, to the priest's Bible? He had been travelling in a train with some other passengers. He had been reading his Bible and nobody said anything. Later the priest left the compartment for a few minutes and when he came back, he saw one of the passengers closing the window. His Bible was gone. They both looked at each other in silence.

The Bible or the Holy Scriptures is a collection of holy books. It is the book of all books. Someone said quite rightly that the Bible is about the history of the world, or of godly providence, from the beginning of the world to the end of the world.

The Bible starts with the book of Genesis and ends with the Apocalypse. Thus the Bible treats the time span from the creation of Heaven and earth to the great illumination, when a new Heaven and a new earth are formed. The Bible consists of 73 books, of which 46 belong to the Old Testament; 6 books and 21 Catholic letters - also called books - belong to the New Testament.

The Holy Bible is the Word of God and its aim is the salvation of everybody. God speaks to us and He rightly expects an answer from us. The Word of God is light, power, word and deed. It is a message and a lesson, therefore also an appeal and a warning to all of us.

The Holy Bible is the book in which we can read how God revealed Himself to man. The heart of the Bible is Jesus Christ. He is the way to God. He is the truth of God. Through Him we can unite with God. We are all invited to come to know the Holy Scriptures better. Saint Jerome says, "Whoever does not know the Holy Scriptures does not know Jesus."

Saint Bonaventura says, "The Holy Bible is the greatest wealth of eternal happiness. In the Holy Bible we find words of eternal life. It was not only written so that we might believe but also so that we might have eternal life, in which we shall see, shall love and shall have all our wishes fulfilled. If all these things are fulfilled, we shall come to know love, which is beyond our knowledge; that way we shall attain perfect fulfilment, which comes from God. The Holy Bible wants to give us an introduction to this perfection. This is the intention and the goal with which we should examine and listen to the Holy Bible. So that we may find the right path according to the Holy Bible and may be able gradually to attain its fruits and its goals, we should start at the beginning, approach the Father of Light with sincere faith and worship Him with all our heart, so that He may grant, through His Son in the Holy Spirit, that we really come to know Jesus Christ. Knowing that He gives us His love, we can, while we love and we perceive and while we are firmly rooted in faith and love, grasp the breadth and the length, the height and the depth of the Holy Bible; we can thus become totally aware of the boundless love of the most Holy Trinity. All the wishes of the saints are addressed to Jesus; in Him we find the wealth and the perfection of all that is genuine and good."

The Bible describes the story of how God saved His people. It tells of how He created the world, made Himself known to man and called man to serve Him. Almost 4,000 years ago, God revealed Himself to Abraham, who lived in Ur in Chaldea. Abraham was the first person who stopped honouring the false Gods and then believed in the one and only true God, Jehovah. The Israelites, God's people, were Abraham's descendants. Through the centuries of history, these people experienced God's love in their many fears and in numerous dangerous situations. God revealed Himself to His people most when He miraculously guided them out of Egyptian slavery to freedom and into the promised land.

All the godly grace bestowed on them was, however, not able to prevent them from running after other gods and so they could not free themselves from sin. Therefore God promised them a Saviour, whom they all awaited with great longing.

This is the Time of Grace

Some 2,000 years later, God fulfilled His promise and sent the Saviour to these people. He was born in Bethlehem, grew up in Nazareth and died in Jerusalem. Through His suffering, His death and His resurrection, He revealed His godly power and love, the victory of life over death. The resurrected Jesus founded the Church through the apostles and the first of the believers; its task today is to proclaim the Kingdom of God, so long as it has not yet arrived. It will arrive at the end of time, however, and this will be the decisive day for the world.

The Queen of Peace, who has been appearing in Medjugorje since 1981, appeals to us wholeheartedly to read the Holy Scriptures at every opportunity. Once she said that every family should pray and read the Holy Scriptures. Some of her messages are as follows:

"Dear children! Today I call upon you to read the Bible every day in your homes. Let it be in a visible place, to encourage you always to read it and to pray." (18.10.1984)

"Dear children! Today is the day on which I give you the message for the parish but not everyone in the parish accepts the message and lives it. I am saddened and I want you to listen to me, dear children, and to live my messages. **Every family must pray and also read the Bible!**" (14.2.1985)

"Dear children! If you pray, God will help you discover the true reason for my coming. Pray, therefore, dear children, and read the Holy Scriptures, so that you discover through them the message for you in my coming here repeatedly!" (25.6.1991)

"Dear children! I again invite you to prayer. You have no excuse to work more because nature still lies in deep sleep. Open yourselves in prayer. Renew prayer in your families. Put Holy Scripture in a visible place in your families, read it, reflect on it and learn how God loves His people. His love shows itself also in present times because He sends me to call you upon the path of salvation." (25.1.1999)

Some good advice on reading the Holy Bible:

Pray before you start to read the Bible.

Contemplate the text you have read and think about it. Keep in your heart what is relevant to you.

Speak to God as to a friend about what is on your mind.

Rest in God, surrender to Him completely, so that His will be done concerning you.

Make the decision to live with the Word of God. Put it into practice. This will give you joy and happiness.

Finish by thanking God for everything.

The Holy Bible helped a doctor to be converted:

A doctor named Marcel tells us his story:
"My mother was a Catholic, a true believer; she always prayed for me, fighting for my earthly and my eternal well-being. She prayed humbly and consistently and continued to hope even when everything seemed hopeless. When I left the house I grew up in, I was an unbeliever. I decided to finish my schooling, got good passes in all my exams and was told by all those who knew me that I had a great future before me. After I became a doctor, I came to know a great many sick people and their sufferings in

the hospital. I saw how some people surrendered to God completely and then endured everything patiently. Where did they get this strength? I did all I could to avoid thinking of God. I thought I had everything and did not need God.

'One day a bricklayer was brought to the hospital. He had fallen from the scaffolding on a building site. His condition was hopeless. We did everything we could to stop him suffering so much. The man knew he was to die soon and was conscious the whole time. I asked him if there was anybody he wanted to see, a relative or a friend. He said he had no-one but wanted to see his landlady because he owed her a little money and wished to pay this debt before he died. We sent for her.

'The bricklayer lived for one week after his accident. I went to see him often and observed that he was really at peace and that his face was radiant, despite his being in a lot of pain and increasingly so. Then he died and I was present when they took him away.

'A nurse asked me, holding a book in her hand, "What shall we do with this, Doctor?" I asked what it was and was told, "It is that poor man's Bible! The woman whose house he lived in, who visited him a few times, brought it to him. That is what he wanted. He kept reading it until he died!"

'I took the Bible and could not believe my eyes. This Bible had once belonged to me. When I left the house I grew up in, I had taken it with me but then sold it. One could still read my name that my mother had written in it. I caught my breath. Could this be true? I told the nurse unemotionally that, as the owner had been alone in the world, I would take it myself.

'This experience was the turning point in my career as a doctor. I took the Bible home and began reading it. I read the part that was marked. Gradually my conscience was awakened and I could not rest until I had found the message of the Gospel, namely that Jesus Christ came into the world to die for us and our sins on the cross and thereby to save us from eternal damnation. This Bible, which I had found again in such an unusual way, is my favourite book of all those in my library.

'After having made a life confession, my life changed completely. The Word of God is powerful and wonderful."

This is the Time of Grace

PART TWO

**"God writes His story with every person.
'You are loved!' is the preface of every story!"**
(Petrus Ceelen)

**"Complete surrender to God's will at a time of afflic-
tion helps us to gather great treasures
for eternity !"**
(Vinzenz Pallotti)

"Everything is transformed through prayer!"
(Basilea Schlink)

What is a Religious Experience?

Today people speak a great deal about religious experiences. What are they?

Here we are dealing with deep spiritual experiences, in which the heart of a person is opened and God's light penetrates it. It is clear to such a person that he comes from God and is to return to Him one day. The person suddenly sees how indescribably important God is. This person also grasps that the Holy Bible is the Word of God. God has become his friend. Grace is palpable. Such a person feels the wish to pray. He finds that his prayer is heard. Everything has changed for him. This person has become different. He has become a true Christian believer. He now speaks about this factually and sensibly. The person's eyes have been opened!

It often happens that such a person receives a gift from the Holy Spirit and can serve others better by means of it. Such an experience is the start of a consciously Christian life. To experience this, one must pray a good deal, namely daily. One should pray at a regular time always.

Why is faith a burden and a torment to some people? It is simply because they have had no religious experiences. They have not yet met the true living God. Alternatively, they did once meet God but they left the correct path through the influence of others. (See, for example, the parable of the seeds that fall onto stony ground, onto thorny ground or onto good ground.)

How does one come to have a religious experience?

There are two very important conditions for a religious experience. First, one must want such an experience with all one's heart; secondly, one must strive for it in prayer with all one's will. To start with, one must wish to be open, sincere, mature and meditative. Simply tell Jesus you long to be perfect and holy, as a saint is; that you wish to have religious experiences and to know the love of God and His proximity, in order to give witness to others. It is very important to read the Holy Bible regularly and be convinced of the shattering experiences of the first Christians. Then, it is necessary to give God first place in one's life and, out of love for God, to repent of all one's sins and sins of omission. Each day one must renounce anew all sin and evil, all dependencies and everything that would separate us from God.

What does it mean to become open to God, so that He can influence us and give us what we need? Many people do not understand this. They are at times even confused. A certain pilgrim keeps coming to mind, who told of how he had to think long and hard about Our Lady's message in which she said we should become open to God. Once it happened that, during prayer, he felt the urge to say to Our Lady, "Blessed Virgin, I do not know how to open my heart and my soul to God. I ask you to take my heart and my whole life and to direct them. I ask of you only that I may learn what it means to become open to God, that is, as you mean it and as you always call upon us to do!"

This young pilgrim did not need to wait long for God to hear his prayer, through the mediation of Our Lady. God gladly hears such prayers. The experience he had cannot be described in words. He tells how, since this spontaneous prayer, he has repeatedly had indescribable, new religious experiences. He declares his heart is now always filled with joy and genuine peace. He no longer finds anything difficult. He feels compelled to pray constantly and to tell others how near God is to us, how much He loves us and how happy He makes us.

Therefore you too should find time to pray every day undisturbed for at least twenty minutes. It must be the most important thing to you in your day! You should not postpone it until later. Pay no attention to either your feelings or your mood; rather, be steadfast and think always of the words of Jesus, that the Father gives us the Holy Spirit when we ask Him for something; besides, it is necessary to believe that we have already received what we want to ask for.

Any era is a time of grace and salvation. Above all, this time in which we are living is a very special time. God is so visibly and obviously at work. He gives His wonderful signs and His appeals to us, as in the cases that we report here.

Prayer in Tongues

A man aged forty from a town in Croatia went to church every day. He asked God in prayer to be allowed to experience God's proximity inwardly. He had never heard of anything to do with experiences of the Holy Spirit. After a few days, at the end of Holy Mass, he felt that his heart was burning and that his tongue was saying prayers that were being given to him from a source outside himself. Later he knew he had received the gift of prayer in other languages.

This is the Time of Grace

The Gift of Prayer

A professor aged thirty-five prayed with others for three weeks for the gift of prayer. Then he experienced something wonderful: great joy, the nearness of God and the gift of prayer. He was now so different that a lot of people asked him what had happened to him.

A question needs to be asked here: why are there so few people who take these wonderful gifts seriously and therefore so many people who do not receive them? It is simply because there are so many who nobody ever spoke to on this subject, so that they know nothing about it. The prayer groups are invited to give witness of what they received from God, in order to make the Church strong.

Let us never forget that prayer always guides us to religious experience. Let us decide every day to accept the Word of God and live according to it! Let Holy Mass, as the Sacrament of all Sacraments, be to us the source of all the graces that Jesus so copiously grants us. An experience of God, a religious experience, can help us to realize what the essence of our faith really is.

A student prayed, "Lord, if You exist, tell me what to do!"

"I was a student in my second semester and was sharing a room with another student in a hostel. One day we began talking about faith. He asked me if I really am a Christian of my own free will. I said I am. After that there came a question I shall never forget: 'Why are you a Christian?' Although I went to Holy Mass regularly and had had religious instruction, I could not answer. Instead of my answering, my fellow student answered, 'You are only officially a Christian!' This made me terribly angry.

I could have beaten him up. I vehemently contradicted his assertion, though I now see it was absolutely right. After that I began thinking more and more intensively about faith and Christianity; I recognized that I was only a Christian because it was customary. My parents were Christians and so I had to belong to the Church too. A few months later, however, there came a decisive moment.

'The following had happened. A woman had done a great deal of harm to my family, with the result that I decided to do her in. What she had done made me angry to such an extreme extent. Then I went to my room and said aloud, **'Lord, if You exist, tell me what to do!'** I said it this way, with the small amount of faith that I had. The next moment, something simply shattered my body. Finally I calmed down but I was then a different person. I was no longer myself! I tried to get angry again and to renew my decision to hate but it was somehow no longer possible. In every way imaginable I tried to regain the state I was in before but I could not! It was as if there was someone in my room. It was as if the Lord Himself was there with me.

'This occurrence had an enormous effect on me and led to my conversion. That was the first religious experience I was aware of. After a time I decided to join a prayer group. At first it was difficult. I did not know the boys and girls in it. Then they began to pray for me in a loud voice. I said my prayers too. I believed that, when we all prayed together this way, God could not refuse us our request. We all wanted the same thing. That is how it turned out, too.

'On Maundy Thursday we were in the chapel. I must admit that I did not want to go. I was preparing for an exam and was scared. I was not yet willing to surrender every-thing to God. I was too calculating but God is, luckily, incalculable. This time He was thinking differently from me. The following night I experienced something. I felt exactly as before, when I was in my room and asked God aloud what to do. Again, but more intensely this time, I had an experience of God. I could perceive His presence. He was very near me and I felt I wanted to thank Him. Something like a current of electricity passed through my body. I began to hold out my arms and then my lips spoke words that sought to express my whole being. It is impossible to say everything I felt. I kept repeating, 'I thank You, oh my Lord God!' I began to understand the significance of prayer and to see all of life quite differently. In case you are interested, I also passed the exam!"

How a young man came to believe:

"I often think of how I used to be. I am a believer but I have only been one for a few months. I was one of the many lads who want to penetrate the secrets of life and try everything out. This was not hard in Zagreb, because the city offers you what they call 'the sweet life' and to me it was simply attractive and irresistible. I had everything I wanted; my world was the discos and nightclubs. Drink-ing, women, all this was completely normal to me. What other youths only dream of lay within my reach.

'The months and years passed and I began to get dis-contented and then, gradually, boredom, dissatisfaction and restlessness invaded my chaotic life. Each day it got worse. I was insecure and felt as if I was in a prison. I was a slave to something that could not be the meaning of my life. There had to be something more valuable and useful in life.

'I used to talk to a boy at that time who had a different way of expressing himself than the one I knew. I therefore realized very soon that he did not think like all the others. We talked for quite a long time and I noticed he had what I lacked. Today I am sure our meeting was no co-incidence!

'This way I gradually came to know the essentials concerning God, faith and a different life. I went to religious instruction with him but I could not break with my old life and the friends I had before (for 'security reasons'). However, I absorbed everything my new friend told me. It was clear to me that this was the right thing for me but it seemed impossible for me to live like that. It is, after all, no good for normal people, I thought. (I am indeed not normal either, but ....)

'I saw no way out of the situation but to set out from the darkness of that time for the new light. I tried and did not manage it. Now I was in the middle of a tug-of-war, between the two fires that both attracted me mercilessly, each one pulling me in its direction. I knew there must be a way out and I even knew on which side; yet it just looked so unattainable.

'One evening I heard, in the religious instruction course, the words: 'What is impossible for man is possible for God!' I had misgivings but deep in my heart I wished that God would make that possible which is not possible for man, namely that I could believe in Him unreservedly!

'After some time I went to a priest. I could simply no longer bear being torn between two things. Something had to change. I decided to go to Confession. It was very hard to express everything but it was even harder to answer the priest's question at the end: 'Do you believe God has now forgiven you for everything?' I was not

This is the Time of Grace

really sure. 'Come, let us pray,' he said, 'so that you feel that the Lord has cleansed you and filled you with His spirit.'

'Then I began to pray. I thought that if God really had forgiven me, I must thank Him and I did so. Then something unusual began to take place within me. My whole burden was suddenly gone, as was my terrible feeling of insecurity! A wonderful current was going through me, which had freed me and begun something new. I fell to my knees for the first time! I was healed!

'Free and cleansed, I went to Holy Mass, to thank God for His grace. My old self had disappeared. Something new had announced itself. It was incomparably stronger than the old self. Since then my life has altered completely. In everyone's eyes I have become a new person, even in the eyes of my former friends."

What is Grace?

Grace is an immeasurably great gift of God. It is God Himself in us, Christ Himself in us. It means an unusual life, a fulfilled life, one filled with happiness, peace, love and graciousness. If we were able to find the happiest person in the world, we could say that he lives his life in grace. This would be a true and perfect life. Total perfection, though, is impossible here in this world. Nevertheless, God does offer the occasional person such a life of happiness. This person then comes to know the joy of life even here on earth, though only for a short time.

There are only two people in history who led a life of true grace, that is, without sin. They are Jesus and Mary. True God for all eternity, Jesus became, when the time was right, a person in Mary's womb. We say of Mary that she had grace in plenitude and was imbued with holiness, imbued with God. She was the one endowed with grace. She was conceived without the original sin with which we are all born. That is why we say Jesus and Mary are a new Adam and a new Eve. They could never commit a sin, i.e. they only ever did good things. We are all invited to lead such a life of grace. We must fight for it every day, in order to win a final victory.

A man named Lucianus was condemned to death for his participation in a conspiracy against the Kaiser. After a long time in a dungeon, he was finally taken to the place of execution, where he was to be hanged. All was in readiness and, while the condemned man was at Confession with the priest, someone called out loud, "The Kaiser has graciously pardoned him!" Everyone was relieved at

108

this decision and rejoiced with Lucianus, who kneeled down, raised his arms toward Heaven and thanked God. Grace is very similar to a royal pardon. Instead of going to one's death, one enters into life; it is, however, not because of one's own merit but a gift out of someone else's goodness. Grace is a great but undeserved gift.

We human beings have, through Adam's disobedience, come to wish to live without God. We live like this condemned man, coming nearer every day to being judged. What is certain is that the hour of death will come one day for everyone. We may then be given grace, i.e. God's gracious pardon, because Jesus sacrificed His life on the cross for us. Then a messenger will come from Heaven and say, "God has pardoned this person!" Instead of going to our death, we shall enter into life.

Grace is life in God. When a person lives honestly, he is in grace, that is, in godly life. Whoever commits a sin or makes a mistake breaks with such a life. The more serious the sin, the farther away grace is. If we then go to Confession, God's grace returns to us. Virtue is the most effective way to make ourselves open to a life in grace.

Virtue opens our hearts to grace!

There was an old man living alone. He was very withdrawn, speaking to and knowing nobody. He had no visitors and also visited nobody. Seeing this, the children rang his doorbell. He did not answer. They threw pebbles at his window. Again there was no answer. In the evening there arose a strong wind; still there was no sign of life from the house and the old man became even more withdrawn. Lying in bed, he pulled the blanket over his head, so as not to hear anything. This went on for days but the sun was watching from behind the clouds and when they finally cleared, the sun said to the wind and the children,

"Stop that! I'll show you how to open the man's windows!" The sun warmed the house; the man soon opened the windows. This is how we become open to grace.

the author speaking to pilgrims

This is the Time of Grace

What Should we Know about our Baptism?

How can we 'reactivate' the graces of our Baptism?

There was a girl of good background who wanted to be baptised. Finally, after thorough preparation, the day came when she was to be baptised. As the baptismal water ran down her forehead and the priest said the words: 'I baptise you in the name of the Father... ', her tears flowed into the baptismal water. At the end of the celebration, she said, "This is the moment I have longed for my whole life. This is the most beautiful and happiest day of my life!"

This young soul received her Baptism with all her heart, with all her soul and with all her strength. Thus, Heaven was opened to her soul and, with the eyes of her soul, she could see Heaven open. Baptism is the sacrament through which God forgives us for our original sin and all the other sins we committed before our Baptism. Moreover, through Baptism we are spared the punishment merited for the sins committed.

Through Baptism, we receive all the graces and the exalted virtues of faith, hope and love. Every baptised person becomes a child of God and an heir of Heaven. The soul of a baptised person is marked with an indelible seal. He has become a member of the Heavenly Kingdom of God on earth (of the Church).

Baptism is the first and most important Sacrament for being saved. Without Baptism there is no God in the soul, that is, no grace.

We should know that, while the priest pours the water over the head of the person being baptised and says the words of Jesus, this is the greatest event in the life of the person. Miracles and more miracles? At this moment, Heaven opens and the Holy Trinity comes down from Heaven, to dwell in the soul of the person. His soul becomes a new Heaven. He becomes a temple of the living God, a brother of Jesus Christ and a child of the Father in Heaven. From this moment, the person belongs to God. A new, divine life of grace begins in him.

This is why we call Baptism 'a new birth' or 'being born again in the spirit'. This new birth of the baptised person consists in shedding the old self and donning the new self, who is created in God's image: cleansed of sin, darkness, wickedness, evil and hell; with true virtue and true holiness.

With virtue and holiness, a person becomes an heir of Heaven, a true child of God. Saint Paul writes: 'In Christ Jesus you are all sons of God, through faith. For as many of you as were baptised into Christ have put on Christ (as a robe).' (Gal. 3, 26-27) With Christ, we share in His being, His worthiness, His holiness, His immortal life; we become 'sons of God'.

A Christian is born twice: he is a child of man and a child of God. A Christian is a 'new being', a holy person, freed of evil and sin.

'We know that our old self was crucified with Him so that the sinful body might be destroyed and we might no longer be enslaved to sin.' (Rom. 6, 6) While Baptism does free us of sin, it is our duty to avoid sin and to endeavour to live our lives with our best brother, with Jesus Christ. We must continually ask ourselves anew whether we are aware of what happened to us at the moment of

112

our Baptism. Unfortunately, many people see being baptised as just a ceremony, not as a truly spiritual state of being.

Baptism should become to us what it was at the time of the New Testament: a state of spiritual life. We must reactivate our Baptism, so that it is effective again. We must repeatedly make ourselves aware of the essential things Baptism gives us: the forgiveness of sins, the gift of the Holy Spirit and a prophetic calling, i.e. we become an instrument of salvation for others.

Baptism means a duty, too, for everyone who is baptised. This means that we accept a duty, with our Baptism, to live according to our faith, i.e. we must live like a child of God; that we should be totally faithful to God and so be able to resemble our Saviour, Jesus Christ. Let us think with His thoughts; let us love God and mankind with the heart of Jesus; let us be witnesses of God's presence in this world. The most important thing is perpetual union with Jesus.

Baptism is an honour, something worthy, great and exalted. It is a great gift, a great grace and a commendation. It means immeasurable happiness; yet it is also a great obligation. This grace, this gift, this faith is something we must keep, tend and realize in the sense that we become converted anew every day, in order constantly to become better, more virtuous, worthier and holier and therefore somewhat more like our dear Lord every day.

We should daily clothe ourselves anew in Jesus Christ. We should be truly Catholic with our heart and with our life. This is not easy. Therefore we must pray and strive every day.

All those who live their Baptism see the world in another light. They are aware that they are not alone. Someone is looking after them, someone who has His great plan with them. The Christian who lives his Baptism sees the other people as his brothers and sisters in Christ, all of us being the children of the one Father in Heaven. Such a Christian considers every encounter with other people as an encounter with Jesus.

Let us recall how Philip, the deacon, baptised the treasurer of the Ethiopian queen. It was after the Holy Spirit had been sent down upon the apostles. More and more people believed in Jesus. The queen's treasurer had been staying in Jerusalem and was now on the way home. He was sitting in his waggon, reading the Holy Scriptures. Near him was Philip, who had been of assistance to the apostles. Philip asked the treasurer if he understood what he was reading. The treasurer answered, "How can I, if nobody guides me?" He asked Philip to get into the waggon and sit with him. There Philip explained to him the Scriptures and what it means to believe in Jesus. Finally they arrived at a place where there was water and the treasurer asked Philip to baptise him. Philip said, "If you believe with all your heart, you can be baptised!" He answered, "I believe Jesus is the son of God!" Philip baptised him then and there and the treasurer continued on his way filled with joy.

What a man named 'Christian' experienced through his Baptism:

There was a man who became a member of the Christian Church very rapidly. He had become a believer and been baptised; now he sat in the first row at church. Some people doubted him and asked him how he could have changed so suddenly, as he had lived like a heathen up to now. Indeed, he could not recite the Creed or the Ten Commandments and he was even unsure of the Lord's Prayer. He explained he had become a new person and had stopped drinking and terrorizing his wife and children, who now waited lovingly for him to come home. He loved them too, did not quarrel any more with them or the neighbours and had stopped swearing. He had not learned much about religion but he knew Jesus had turned his life around completely, which had been the best catechism. Holy Mass had become an encounter with Jesus the resurrected!

God is Extremely Effective Today

Witness Numerous Healings, Conversions and Vocations!

**"You created us for You, O Lord,
and our heart is restless until it rests in Thee!"**
(Saint Augustine)

**"Whoever does the will of the Father
comes to know and love God Himself!"**
(Edith Stein)

**"Nothing can happen to me that
God does not want!"**
(Thomas Morus)

A girl student was converted in a moving way:

Brought up in a Catholic family, this girl had grown further and further away from God. She had lived in a sinful state for years and had stopped going to church to receive the Sacraments. She had lost her faith. It had been ruined through her contact with bad company. She was consuming hashish and alcohol.

Somehow she arrived in Medjugorje, though not even she knew why. She was not interested in the apparitions, since she did not believe in God. The first few days were difficult for her. Then, in the apparition chapel, a miracle took place. It was Maundy Thursday. She finds it hard to describe in words what happened at a certain moment when a great force made her kneel down.

She says: "There were moments of inner joy. I believe! There is a God! He became a person! He changes into bread! I became conscious that He was present, present in the consecrated host. I could not help weeping with happiness. I cried a lot in the next few days; yet at the same time I felt God's merciful love. On Easter Saturday I went to Confession and then I celebrated Easter on the Sunday. I am risen from the dead.

'I was blissfully happy for months afterwards, especially at Holy Mass or during prayer; even if I say the name of Jesus or Mary or simply think of them, the happiness comes into my heart. My life is so different, as I could never have imagined. I have given up smoking, drinking and listening to rock music.

'I am happy. To me, Holy Mass is the best and most important part of the day. It makes me happiest. The King of kings comes into my heart. He loves me and through me all those I meet. I am sure that God will, through Mary, continue to guide me."

Indeed, it is so. This girl answered the call of God and He has made her really holy. She has been living in the community of the 'Oasis of Peace' for over ten years. This community is one of the major fruits that have come through Medjugorje. Eight hours of prayer a day is normal here. Every branch of the community has perpetual adoration of Jesus in the Most Holy Sacrament.

This way they serve Jesus through Mary and live the Gospel of Jesus.

An Italian was converted miraculously:

An Italian man tells us how he was converted in Medjugorje. His story shows how powerful God's presence is in this place of pilgrimage.

"My friends had told me of Medjugorje and the miraculous events there. In December 1988 I was privileged enough to experience a miraculous turning point in life myself. If I say I was the greatest sinner of all, you will surely think this an exaggeration. I do not know if there is a sin that I had not committed. I was also a drug addict. Nothing seemed to give me any joy or happiness, least of all sin itself. Absolutely everything put me under terrible, unbearable pressure, so that finally I even wanted to kill myself.

'There, however, I realized why I was alive. In that place where Our Lady appears and Heaven is open, I prayed as follows: "Blessed Virgin, Mother of Jesus and my Mother, I believe you are appearing here. You came here for my sake too. I beg you to commend me to your Son.

Ask for the grace of conversion for me. I am fully convinced that your godly Son will hear your request as mediator for me. I cannot go on living like this; this is not a life. Mother, if you do not help me, I do not know any way out of this; I cannot go back. Queen of Peace, ask for peace for me from your Son. Help me, I implore you!"

'Then there was emptiness; I knew nothing more, not another step. Suddenly I was seized by an urge to confess. I found an Italian priest without any difficulty and kneeled before him as a successor of Christ. What happened at these moments of grace and healing is known only to the dear Lord, the priest and myself. I will never forget this encounter. It is very hard to describe the circumstances in plain words and also do justice to the situation. I can only say I experienced personally that God is love that heals, sets you free and forgives you, renews and saves you. I have been in this state of grace for some years now. Truly, there is nothing more delightful and fulfilling in this world."

Witness of Medjugorje given movingly by a young priest:

A young priest from America was at a conference on Medjugorje in 1994 and gave witness of the following moving experience. Even as a schoolboy he had got into bad company and become addicted to drugs. Other problems were soon added to this wretched state of existence. He began to neglect school and go home late. When his father found out he was a drug addict, he was beside himself and tried to get him off the drugs immediately.

These efforts were in vain. Finally the father angrily threw him out of the house into the street, to which the son had belonged for a long time anyhow. His condition worsened markedly. Hearing, from his remaining friends, how the Blessed Virgin was appearing in Medjugorje and helping people with problems, he felt straight away that he wanted to go there. Of course he could not afford such a trip; he did not even have enough money for drugs any more. When friends of his father's heard of this, they paid for a trip to Medjugorje for him.

He quickly joined a group of pilgrims going to Medjugorje. On arriving he observed everything that was happening around him. He saw people who were starting to pray fervently. Others were going to Confession. After giving it some thought, he decided that a confession would do him good too. It did, for he was filled with great joy afterwards and decided to live in future without drugs.

On the way home, it occurred to him that he could become a priest. At home he went to his bishop and told him of this wish. The bishop asked him all sorts of questions in a lengthy discussion. He did not dare reveal to the bishop, however, that he had taken drugs, for fear of being refused. The bishop finally promised him that he could join the seminary for priests and realize his wish. After taking the course of studies and passing the exams, he was consecrated as a priest. Soon afterwards, the same bishop gave him the task of bringing the Gospel to young people, especially to drug addicts, the same group as he had belonged to once himself.

After giving witness of his conversion, the young priest raised his hands to Heaven, and said, "Look at these hands! They used to hold drugs and distribute them to others too. Today they hold Jesus and give **Him** to the

120

others!" Everything about him showed that he had become a happy person and was now at peace within himself.

"Dear children! Behold, also today I want to call you to start living a new life as of today. Dear children, I want you to comprehend that God has chosen each one of you, in order to use you in His great plan for the salvation of mankind. You are not able to comprehend how great your role is in God's design. Therefore, dear children, pray so that in prayer you may be able to comprehend what God's plan is in your regard. I am with you in order that you may be able to bring it about in all its fullness. Thank you for having responded to my call." (25.1.1987)

"Dear children! Today also I am calling you to prayer. You know, dear children, that God grants special graces in prayer. Therefore, seek and pray in order that you may be able to comprehend all that I am giving here. I call you, dear children, to prayer with the heart. You know that without prayer you cannot comprehend all that God is planning through each one of you. Therefore, pray! I desire that through each one of you God's plan may be fulfilled, that all which God has planted in your heart may keep on growing. So pray that God's blessing may protect each one of you from all the evil that is threatening you. I bless you, dear children. Thank you for having responded to my call." (25.4.1987)

In Medjugorje Regina was converted and answered God's call:

Sister Regina Schmidt gives witness of her profound and unforgettable experiences of faith and of Jesus and Mary in the church at Medjugorje and on the Mount of the Cross. She was given the assurance that God is the dearest Father and that we are allowed to be His children.

She admits that God had called her through Mary much earlier but then she was a long way from Him and the life of a Christian who gives witness. She finally went to Medjugorje to please her boyfriend. He had told her that Mary, the Queen of Peace, was appearing there and helping everyone along life's path. Regina was thrilled and was in no doubt the apparitions were genuine. Then, later, when they were engaged to be married, they returned to this place of grace. She declares they felt they were in Paradise when they were in Medjugorje. They had made their plans and had decided to get married there too. God, however, had His own plans for them.

When she arrived home from Medjugorje, Regina began to lead a different life and others noticed this. What had been important to her, like the disco and television, did not interest her any longer. Her parents feared she had fallen into the hands of a sect. She began to pray more and more, especially the Rosary, also joining a prayer group. When she read in a book that Our Lady is joyful when someone enters a religious community, Regina wished with all her heart to give this joy to the dear Blessed Mother.

The question was how to do this. How could she realize such a thing? Her prayers became more and more fervent. Then, when Pentecost came, God gave her enlightenment as to which community He wanted her to

122

enter. At this moment she felt such ardent love for Jesus and entrusted herself to God completely. Then, however, she had doubts about this wish of hers, in case God might be offended at her breaking her promise of marriage. She asked Our Lady to intercede and appeal to her godly Son, so as to be able to fulfil God's will.

When she finally spoke to Josef, her betrothed, of her wish, he was most understanding about it and was prepared to waive the promise she had given him, to leave her free for Jesus. It was not easy for him but he did not complain. For fifteen years now, Sister Regina has been with the Merciful Sisters of St Vincent de Paul. Her former betrothed, Josef Lackstaetter, was consecrated as a priest in 1995 and joined the Benedictine Order.

Sister Regina declares that the messages of the Blessed Virgin are an extremely great source of grace, motivation and help in always remaining true to her vocation and to the grace of God.

Eugenio M. Pirovano's dramatic experiences:

Father Pirovano is a priest and head of an Italian religious community but he himself lives and works, however, in Brazil. He says he had heard of Medjugorje through a young man in his parish in Sao Paolo. The visionary Marija had visited a neighbouring congregation and spoken about the events in Medjugorje. Father Pirovano had not invited her to his parish because he simply could not believe that Our Lady would appear in a small, unknown village and a Communist one at that!

He again heard of Medjugorje, when he went back to Italy to pursue some further studies. The time in Italy was, unfortunately, a difficult one. Father Pirovano finally found out that he was about to be accused of something quite serious, a misdemeanour. This affected him deeply.

He tells us, "Then my father became seriously ill and I was told he had but three months to live. I broke off my studies and went to Milan to be with him for the remaining time. Shortly before my father died, my brother was arrested, because one of his employees had embezzled a lot of money. This was a great shock to me and I withdrew to one of our houses. It was soon clear that these accusations were affecting me considerably. Then every circumstance started to go against me and my superior believed those who were accusing me. It was unthinkable that I could remain a priest...."

Then Father Pirovano was invited to Medjugorje. He did not want to go, as he did not believe in the apparitions. Two friends, who knew his situation, finally persuaded him to go there. On arriving, he learned that Ivan, one of the visionaries, was to have an apparition on the Mount of the Cross and all the other pilgrims were pleased; only he was completely uninterested.

About 6 o'clock in the evening, a young pilgrim asked him to set out for the Mount of the Cross, in order to pray the Fourteen Stations on the way up. The priest refused, because the youth had come on account of the apparition. The priest's refusal to say the prayers made the youth very angry and the two of them had a slight argument. Then, when they were all at dinner, someone drew the others' attention to the cross on top of the mountain, because a wonderful star could be seen there. Everyone felt it was a sign, calling them to prayer. The priest immediately asked the people to go to the mountain and pray the Stations of the Cross with him.

He says, "I urged everybody to kneel at every single station. I, however, intentionally remained standing and prayed at length, so that the people's knees would hurt. It had been raining heavily. Suddenly, though, I noticed my coat was completely dry, as if it had not rained at all; that startled me. Then I shortened the prayers at each station. Deep in my heart I was complaining to God and His Mother about my situation. Every so often, I touched the coats of the others to see if they were wet, which they were. The only dry one was mine."

When the group arrived at the top of the mountain, the rain stopped, though all around them it continued to fall. The priest asked a few people to lead the prayers, while he himself prayed as follows: "Blessed Virgin, I do not know if you are appearing here. If you are, I want you to know that I am not only a good priest but also a really good one! I shall tell you all my good points. I pray the breviary every day, I am devoted to You, I preach, I believe, I spread the Gospel and now I have been unjustly accused by my fellow priests. Is that the thanks I get for all the good things I do?"

The next day he went to the Mount of Apparitions to pray the Rosary. He sat down by a cross, so as to be some distance from the other people. A man came and joined him, whom he never saw again after that. This man asked him if he was Eugenio from Brazil. The priest became suspicious and thought this must be a policeman; the Communist regime was still in power. When he asked this man who he was, he replied, "Who I am is not important but I have a message from our Lord Jesus Christ for you, a message through the mediation of Our Lady. It refers to your prayer on the Mount of the Cross yesterday and, if you wish to hear it, I shall tell you what it is."

The priest agreed and was told, "Our Lady says you are a really good priest but you should not despise the simple faith of the people, the way you did regarding the lad in your parish!" (The priest knew that, apart from the lad and himself, no-one knew he had forbidden the lad to speak about Medjugorje.) The man continued, "Your father is in Paradise with your mother; your brother will be let out of prison. Our Lady has a task for you. Numerous people have written to Medjugorje to say they would like to have a really good priest for their parish. Our Lady has chosen you to go to Brazil and take over this parish!" The man added, "Because you still do not believe, Our Lady will give you a sign."

The priest did not want to listen any longer but to be left in peace. In the crowd he saw another priest and asked him to hear the confession of his whole life, adding, "You who believe in the apparitions of Our Lady here, tell her I do not need any further sign of her presence here."

The next thing was that a bus full of pilgrims without a priest arrived. These people asked him to pray the Stations of the Cross with them on the Mount of the Cross and he gladly agreed to do so. At the third station, a young man started to cry, which startled and interrupted the priest. Later the young man came and apologized to the priest and explained that he had seen his sins as in a film; he had then seen further sins of his and could not stop crying and feeling remorse for his sins. The priest wondered how many sins the young man had committed, as he just could not settle down.

The young man also said, "When you finished the prayers, I heard in my heart the voice of Our Lady saying, 'You are forgiven your sins but go to a priest so that you

This is the Time of Grace

get the forgiveness of the Church.' " Father Pirovano then heard a good confession from the young man and gave him absolution. He soon came back to the priest, however, and added, "I am a drug addict and have used heroine." Then he took the drugs out of his pocket and threw them away, adding, "Father, I am healed and I am the sign Our Lady promised you."

The priest tells us, "This touched me profoundly and from that moment I was inwardly different. From now on I shall go to Medjugorje every year, even during the war." He has since founded the religious community named 'The Followers of Jesus in Honour of the Father'. The local bishop has confirmed this community, which looks after abandoned children and those living on the streets, just as Our Lady wished. Children come to know the wonderful signs of love and of God's goodness. The Pope, too, has given this community his blessing.

Father Pirovano concludes, "In Medjugorje I learned to pray and to be obedient. I learned to listen. There I understood that, when we pray with our heart, Our Lady guides us, so that we recognize the path of holiness and live our life with crucified Jesus."

An IRA terrorist from Belfast was converted:

An Irishman gave witness as follows: "When I was two years old, our house was attacked by bands of loyalists and bombed. Numerous people I had known when I was young were killed by soldiers and I wanted revenge! I joined the Irish Republican Army in 1978, to fight for a united homeland. It was my task to murder British soldiers and police surreptitiously.

'I was arrested six years later and sentenced to twelve years' imprisonment. In prison I heard of the events in Medjugorje through Father Paddy Kenny. In the quiet of my cell, I occupied myself with the messages of Our Lady and felt a great longing for this place of grace. Then in 1988 I was released earlier than planned and went to Medjugorje immediately. I stayed there for three months and during this time I was filled with profound peace and love.

'My life is now totally different and, having returned to Ireland, I have founded a great many prayer groups in recent years. I now guide young people to Jesus and Mary, to give new meaning to their shattered lives.

'Today I know this: God is love and we are all brothers and sisters in Him!"

Veronica Knox was healed:

The idea that she should go to Medjugorje was given to Veronica Knox by Jesus Himself and there she was indeed healed of her poor eyesight. It was in 1998 and she had suffered from defects in the retina of both eyes all the 43 years of her life. After eight operations, she could still see virtually nothing, at most the difference between light and darkness.

In her own words: "One morning I was saying my daily prayers, particularly the Rosary. My eyes were closed and suddenly I saw Jesus before me; He was surrounded by bright light. I felt warmth inwardly and especially in my face. He said, 'Come and pray with me!' I told Him that the light was so strong that I could not see anything. Jesus returned, 'I shall show you a light that is going to guide your way!' I stood up and approached this light. In it I saw a mountain with a big cross on top. Jesus

This is the Time of Grace

was no longer visible. I also saw a church with two big towers and three big windows. I told Him I did not know where we were, though I had been to Lourdes and Fatima. Jesus said, 'This is Medjugorje!' and showed me the whole place. Then He was gone. I wept but I wrote down what had happened so as not to forget any of it. I told my husband of it and he could not make out what it was that I was telling him. I repeated that I had been in Medjugorje that morning with Jesus. He immediately decided to go and buy tickets so that we could go to Medjugorje. When I arrived there, I found everything just as Jesus had shown it to me.

'When we finally found the blue cross there, I had an unusual experience. While praying before this cross, I suddenly glimpsed Our Lady for a moment with her arms outstretched and I felt indescribable peace. Then we were at Vicka's house one morning and heard her give witness, along with a large crowd of pilgrims. Afterwards, she came over to me and laid her hand over my eyes and prayed. I did not understand her prayer but at the end of it, my sight had improved and was found to be one hundred per cent in the right eye. I said, 'Thank You, Jesus!' I also prayed a lot for my daughter, so that she might start going to church again and also have her child baptised and, to my delight, this grace was granted to us. She telephoned me and told me she would do just that.

'I can say that my life is completely different now. The most important thing in my life is to give witness of Jesus and Mary. I teach others to pray the Rosary and I tell of the messages of the Queen of Peace. They are messages of love, peace, conversion and fasting. We should lead a life in which we worthily receive the Sacraments. My heart is filled with love for Jesus, Mary and all of humanity."

A young American was converted in prison:

Sentenced to 20 years in prison for murder, a young American was watching a video of the events in Medjugorje when, at the moment of the apparition, he also saw a lovely, ethereal and beautiful woman. She said to him, "My dear son, I am your Mother; be converted!"
He did not know who this woman in the white robe was and what her words 'Be converted!' meant. None of his friends could give him an answer. The prison chaplain, however, was able to help him a great deal and spoke with him at length. Finally the young man wanted to become a Catholic. He was given thorough preparation and then received the Sacraments. He had also understood what an important part prayer plays in the life of a Catholic.
Then he created numerous prayer groups in the prison. Everyone saw a great change in him and this contributed to his release from prison twelve years earlier than expected. Now he travels about and gives talks at conferences on how God is active nowadays and how great God's love is. This way, the young man helps many others to convert and to begin a new life.

A French woman was healed in Medjugorje:

A married couple from Paris went for a pilgrimage to Medjugorje, the wife having had a tumour in her throat for seven years. She could no longer speak and could only eat pureed food. He husband said they had now decided to seek consolation in Medjugorje, having done the same in many other places of pilgrimage too.

Her healing took place on 7 October, the day the Church celebrates Our Lady of the Rosary. She and her husband

This is the Time of Grace

had prayed the whole day. Then, in the afternoon, she was able to eat a sandwich and by evening, after Holy Mass and the other prayers, she was able to eat normally like everybody else. She began to speak again too!

Now it was the other pilgrims' turn to be speechless; they were amazed and saw it was a miracle. The woman who was healed wondered at it too and asked what Medjugorje might be. Her husband provided all the medical documents to prove the healing and gave witness that his wife had been healed through the intercession of the Queen of Peace.

Diana Basile was healed of multiple sclerosis:

Despite the best and most modern treatment at Milan Hospital, Diana Basile was becoming weaker and her health was deteriorating by the day. One of her eyes had already failed. The doctors were by this stage unable to treat her further and all they could do was to try to stave off the worst outcome. In this seemingly hopeless situation, Diana heard of Medjugorje and felt an ardent wish to go there, to ask Our Lady to obtain healing for her.

In Medjugorje she was able to be present at an apparition with the help of friends. At that time they took place in the church and she was praying quietly when the apparition started. She immediately felt better and after it she could stand up unaided, which she had not been able to do before it.

She now attended Holy Mass, which was just beginning in the church. Those who knew her could hardly believe what they saw and next day she walked twelve kilometres from her hotel to the Mount of Apparitions, to thank the dear Blessed Virgin, who had been instrumental in her healing.

After she returned to Milan, the doctors could not understand how Diana had regained her health so they decided to check the records of her illness, her therapy and her new state of health. They compiled a 142-page report, confirming the earlier diagnosis and the present state of health. The 25 medical experts have confirmed all the facts of her case and that she is now completely free of the disease. The techniques of medicine could not have cured her. She is now still completely free of the illness. It is as if she had never been ill.

Rita Klaus was miraculously healed:

For 26 years, Rita Klaus, an American, had been suffering from multiple sclerosis and not even the best treatment had been able to heal her. Her condition was even worsening, until there came an unforeseen change for the better.

She describes it as follows: "It was 18 June 1986, a Wednesday, and I had prayed my daily Rosary. Suddenly I felt I really wanted to ask Jesus for healing through the intercession of Our Lady of Medjugorje. In my heart I said to her, 'Dear Mother, Queen of Peace, I believe that you are appearing to the visionaries in Medjugorje. I beg of you, please ask your Son to heal me, in every way I need. Your Son said faith can move mountains. I believe and I ask you to help me overcome any lack of belief.'

'After asking our Mother Mary to intercede for me, I felt as if an electric shock was going through me. I had felt such sensations before but they were always like an unpleasant jolt. This time it was quite different: it was

132

pleasant, mild and gentle. I went to my bedroom on the ground floor, to take off my callipers. As I was doing so, I noticed that my legs somehow looked strange. Then I realized they were normal again. I took off the callipers and, using my crutches, I went to the stairs leading to the upper floors. I thought to myself that, if I was cured, I would be able to walk up the stairs. I did walk up the stairs! Then I ran through the whole flat, laughing and crying with joy!

'On 23 June I was examined by my doctor at Hamarville Rehabilitation Hospital in Pittsburgh. There was no trace of the MS left. All my reflexes were normal and the trembling was gone. The doctor told me I had been reborn and now had the chance of a new life. He suggested that on the way home I go into a church and give thanks to God. I am completely healed!"

Rita later went to Medjugorje to thank the dear Blessed Virgin Mary. She took with her a report 100 pages long on her illness and subsequent cure. Her miraculous healing has brought about numerous conversions, as many as thirty, among her relatives and friends.

Nancy Lauer was healed:

Nancy Lauer, an American, had had a hard life, one of suffering and torment including four serious operations. She says something attracted her very strongly to Medjugorje. During an apparition in the choir loft of the church, she prayed, "Blessed Virgin, I know you love me and I love you too. Help me to fulfil God's will! I can bear my illness with God's help. I beg you always to help me to do God's will." Nancy prayed for a child, too, suffering from cancer. After the apparition she was completely healed.

Regina was cured of an incurable illness!

When Regina was five, the doctors found a malignant tumour in her left kidney. In her lung and her liver there were metastases, too. The left kidney was removed immediately and chemotherapy was begun.

A new tumour, however, started growing in the same area. The course of chemotherapy was increased to a maximum dose. As a result, Regina's heart was severely damaged. The doctors said this would inevitably lead to her death; only a heart transplant might save her.

Regina was brave and cheerful and said, "If I die, I know where I will go and there I will feel fine!" Her parents felt greatly comforted by these words. It was now easier for them to say, "Lord, Thy will be done!" They were now prepared to accept anything God gave them, even her death, and refused permission for a heart transplant. Their child's condition was so serious that the doctors told them their child could even die at home.

Meanwhile their petition was told to the Medjugorje visionaries and they presented it to Our Lady. The parents took Regina to a healing service in Wuerzburg (Germany), held by Father Klaus Mueller, who gave her a blessing and prayed for her recovery. From the very day the parents accepted that God's will be done, their critically ill child's condition improved by the hour.

Seven years have since passed and Regina, who regained her health, now says, "I am very well! Jesus died for us and redeemed the world. He performed miracles and healed the sick. Jesus is the Son of God, who loves humanity and wants us all to go to Heaven. We can have faith in Him; we should pray a lot and go to church.

This is the Time of Grace

Above all we should love Jesus!" Her father says, "We have six children. Since her healing, Regina has been the healthiest of all of them and has never been ill again!" Regina shows no sign of the deadly illness. All the metastases disappeared and her heart is normal again. God intervened and showed us His omnipotence.

Colleen Willard's miraculous healing

An American woman from Chicago, Colleen Willard, had a brain tumour which was incurable and caused her terrible suffering. She had lost weight drastically. She could no longer climb the stairs to her room or get to the bathroom unaided. Any contact with her skin caused her unbearable pain. Her husband John continued to work, to make a living for his family, while their twenty-one-year old son stayed home in order to take care of her.

Prayer was Colleen's only refuge. Despite her difficult situation, she tried to help others and worked voluntarily for the society 'Saint Clara, Help of the Poor'. She was one of the best workers, doing telephone duty (as far as her voice allowed it) to collect donations for Bosnian war victims.

One day Colleen heard of Medjugorje and immediately wanted to go there, yet she knew she could not manage the trip. Moreover, the family did not have the financial means, because of the numerous medical bills. She just thought to herself, "I do not want to go there to be cured but to experience the presence of Our Lady in this holy place."

Her family prayed fervently that she would be able somehow to make this pilgrimage and God granted them His grace. The trip became possible and she was able to travel first class. During the journey she had to take pain killers every two hours but she was joyful and thanked God for everything.

The morning after her arrival, Colleen was taken in her wheelchair to meet one of the visionaries, which turned out to be difficult, as a great many people were crowding around the visionary. Just as the situation seemed to Colleen to be getting critical, the visionary made her way through the crowd to her, put her arm round her and prayed for her.

Then Colleen was taken to Holy Mass in the church, where her husband wheeled her to the front. As the priest began to consecrate the host, she suddenly heard the voice of the Virgin Mary: "My daughter, surrender completely to God the Father! Surrender completely to my betrothed, the Holy Spirit! Surrender to my Son Jesus! Surrender now completely!" She answered, "Yes, I surrender completely! Entirely for the honour of Heaven, entirely for the honour of God!"

At that moment, Colleen felt a tingling in her legs and noticed straight away that something had happened to her. Towards the end of Mass she knew she was healed. She stood up out of the wheelchair and was able to walk out of the church, without difficulty and unaided.

When Colleen returned home, she went to see the doctors treating her at the Mayo Clinic. At first they could not understand how she was healed. She was examined in various ways, which confirmed that she was cured. Finally a doctor said to her, "Your cure is the third one achieved through Medjugorje!"

This is the Time of Grace

Katharina, a long-suffering victim of MS, was healed in Medjugorje:

A lady called Katharina was always in great pain from multiple sclerosis. She could scarcely take a few steps, had no strength in her hands and feet and was mostly in a wheelchair.

Her daughter took her to Medjugorje with a group of pilgrims, who carried her up the Mount of Apparitions and the Mount of the Cross. One Friday, she was in the church in her wheelchair, very near the altar. The church was very crowded. Then God worked a miracle for this very religious lady.

Katharina had prayed a lot for her family and made sacrifices for them. There were problems in the family. Her son was having a relationship with a girl who was now expecting a child; they had both decided on an abortion. Her husband was terminally ill with cancer.

Now Katharina put her whole life in Jesus' hands. She prayed, "Dearest Mother and Queen of Peace, I am here where you are appearing. Please help me to do the will of God and to obey! In my family there are difficulties but I believe God can change everything for the better if one loves Him and asks Him humbly for help. Lord, may Your will be done regarding me, my husband and my son!"

Suddenly and unexpectedly, the miracle took place. She was healed that very moment. The same evening she climbed the steep, rocky Mount of the Cross and there thanked Jesus and Mary.

On arriving home, her son told her he was going to marry his girlfriend and they were going to keep the baby. Her husband told her he had had another medical examination and there was no sign of cancer left. This news had been given him by the same doctor who had told her that her husband did not have much longer to live. At the time, she had reacted by saying, "I have faith in another doctor." She meant God.

Such miracles show us how God is active in our times too! Life is unthinkable without Him, despite the fact that some people do not know Him. He is our creator. There is nothing God could not do if He wanted to. We should be true believers in Him and trust in Him. We should never forget that He is present. Our powerful intercessor, Mary, has come into our midst and wishes to help us. She wishes to guide us to her Son. Let us allow her to do so. We can then experience miracles.

Conversion at the last moment:

It was a long time ago, 1927, when this case of a young, twenty year-old man was recorded in Augsburg, Germany. He lay on his bed at home, dying of a fatal illness.

On the wall hung a simple picture of the Sacred Heart of Jesus. His eye often fell on the picture and yet it did not evoke in him any good, pious thoughts at all, rather the opposite. No, he was not a believer. He was prone to utter curses and blasphemies.

His good mother was very worried. She must have sensed it was his last day on earth. Tearfully she implored God for mercy for her lost son. An appeal to the young man himself to ask God even once to forgive him his sinful life was greeted with swear words. Then he shouted, "Let the devil come and get me and you too whenever he likes!"

This is the Time of Grace

Just then, the bell of the nearby church started ringing. It was time for Holy Mass. The mother glanced imploringly at the picture of Jesus' Sacred Heart. Then she hurried to church, kneeled down and wept bitterly. At the moment of the transubstantiation, she begged the Lord with all her heart for help for her poor son, saying several times the words of the repentant felon, "Jesus, remember me when You come into Your Kingdom." (Luke 23, 42) She also offered up the Precious Blood of the Saviour for the salvation of her son.

After Mass the woman set off for home, comforted yet afraid of being sworn at again by her son. On the contrary, what a difference there was! He said to her, "Mother, how badly I have treated you all the years and what a sinful life I have led! A quarter of an hour ago, it was as if this picture on the wall looked at me and told me that, if I repented, my sins would be forgiven!"

He begged her to have a priest come to the house. Half an hour later, he confessed the sins of his life, his cheeks bathed in copious tears of true repentance. Straight after that, he was given the Last Sacrament.

When the late afternoon sunrays reached his room, they lit up the peaceful face of one who had passed away. There before the picture of the Sacred Heart knelt his mother, rapt in prayers of gratitude to the Saviour for the mercy of His Most Holy Heart.

God saved Andy from an early death:

A smoker from the age of fourteen, Andy was smoking three packets a day. His doctor told him that, if he did not stop smoking, he would be digging his own grave.

While doing military service, Andy one day heard a talk given by the army priest, who told the soldiers that the God of our fathers is the living God who hears prayers every day. Afterwards Andy went to the priest and asked him if he really believed what he had told them. The priest replied that he certainly did. Andy asked him to confirm that he believed God would hear him instantly if he prayed to him. The priest confirmed it. Then Andy told him of his smoking problem and the doctor's prognosis. The priest said that in his case smoking was a sin. Andy asked him to pray to God for a solution to the problem. The priest laid his hand on Andy's shoulder and prayed, "Lord, help Andy and free him from this dependency; never let him smoke again!"

When Andy left the priest, he thought to himself that it would be a simple matter to prove the priest wrong. He only had to smoke a cigarette. Soon he went and lit one up secretly. After the first puff, he felt nauseous and had to be sick. Thinking it was a coincidence, he tried a cigarette again later. However, the same thing happened. Every time he tried to smoke, he could not and he was overcome with nausea.

Andy reported to the priest what had happened and both were very happy. The next thing was that Andy asked the priest to ask God to forgive him his sins. Andy was then able to accept Christ as his true Saviour. From then on, his life was joyous and meaningful.

The Lord not only wants to help us with our problems; He also wants to set us on the path to eternal happiness. A problem put into the Lord's hands can be the start of a true life in God. We should never hesitate to confide in the Lord! He is the most loving Father and He is infallible.

God granted Steve a new life:

Steve, a young man from Canada, spent his teenage years in the chaos of alcohol and drugs. He stole to fund his addictions. This life, however, came to disgust him more and more.

His parents had told him of the wonderful things happening in Medjugorje and offered to take him there, as they organized pilgrimages to this oasis of peace, as it is called. He was not interested in it and refused for a long time until something changed his mind and he agreed to go with them.

His first impression of Medjugorje was that the people there were happy and uncomplicated and so he joined in. He knew no prayers but quickly learned them and was surprised to find it easy to pray. When his group went to the Mount of the Cross, he joined in praying the Fourteen Stations but at the twelfth station he began to cry and could not stop. A voice from his group said, "One of us has been cured of drug addiction and this is a great conversion which God has granted."

This gave Steve great joy and peace. He thanked God immediately for His help and His mercy. Later he realized the significance of the twelfth station: Jesus came to die for our sins, so that we may be freed of them and live. This was a rebirth for Steve, whose heart was then open to God and whose faith gained in strength daily. After making a confession of his whole life, Steve could sense the presence of Our Lady and felt that he was loved by God.

He realized that, at home, he would have to start a new life and end his association with people who had been important to him. It was not easy for him to leave the girlfriend with whom he had been living but he knew this way of life was offensive to God. Marriage is a Sacrament, is worthy of God's blessing and is permanent; a casual relationship is unworthy and is not part of God's plan. Steve's rebirth meant that he now saw that it is right to live according to God's commandments. They were not put in place by chance or to deprive us of something good; they protect us from what is bad.

It is Steve's wish to become a priest. He recognizes what graces God has given him and he wants only to do God's will. He thanks the Lord for all that he has received and will receive from Him as a priest.

Tibor found the meaning of his life in Medjugorje:

Seventeen years old and from Prague, Tibor had been unhappy all his youth. He was only one year old when he was sent to a children's home, his father having died and his mother having been sentenced to twelve years in prison. In the home, he felt isolated and rejected; people used to mock him. When his mother came out of prison, she moved in with a man who was an alcoholic and often beat her. Tibor had begun to hate people and was thrown out of the house by his mother, having gone to live with her. He then went to another home for young people but became mentally ill. Once he cut his veins but the doctors saved him. Another time he swallowed a vast number of tablets but brought them up again, which saved his life. Yet again he tried to kill himself: he stabbed himself in the abdomen with a long knife but was again saved.

The next move was to a psychological hospital but it proved to be the turning point for Tibor. A doctor, who was religious, had him sent to live with a religious family, where he was looked after free of charge.

The family had him baptised as a Catholic and his foster mother prayed a lot for him. He had complexes and suffered from loneliness and severe depression. Through this family, Tibor went for a pilgrimage to the place of great healing, Medjugorje. On arriving, he just sat outside the church and felt unsure and unhappy. However, some pilgrims came over and talked to him, which made him feel at peace and even very happy. His depression was not yet over and he cried repeatedly, even reproaching Our Lady with refusing to comfort him. Then a priest laid his hands on Tibor's head and the blessing he received worked wonders. He felt relieved and happy and a genuine love for his fellow beings filled his heart.

On the Mount of Apparitions, Tibor wept a great deal but slowly went towards the big cross and there placed his hand on the feet of crucified Jesus. A strong gust of wind suddenly began to blow the cross back and forth. It seemed to awaken something in Tibor, for he realized he would like to become a priest. He is no longer lonely, he says. He has found God and Our Lady. He likes going to Medjugorje, where he prays for his vocation and his total dedication to God. His wish to guide others to God and the faith grows ever stronger. Tibor's heart is now healed.

A man from the Lake Constance area

A man from the area of Lake Constance tells of his sudden conversion through the events in Medjugorje.

"Since our wedding I had never been to a Catholic church again. Then when our children went to their first Holy Communion, I went to the church for their sakes. For about eleven years I had not seen a church from the inside!

'My wife was due to be baptised in Medjugorje and so she asked me to accompany her there. When I first went into the church in Medjugorje I went in only as far as the inner glass doors, while my wife and my mother went right inside.

'At this door I suddenly turned round and went outside again. Even today I still do not know the reason. Outside I went along the side of the church, where people were going to Confession. I did not even realize what the people were doing there; I simply observed them. Then I saw the notice-boards with names of different languages on them and among them I saw 'German'. Without intending to, I joined the line of people waiting for Confession in German. I had the feeling someone had guided me here. Then I made my confession.

'After confessing, I felt as if a weight had fallen from my heart. I was very relieved and happy, especially because I was able to be in this holy place and could also have Holy Communion.

'During evening Mass I saw a miracle experienced by a ten-year old girl, who had been blind for seven years. I was deeply impressed. God had shown me the right way again!

'My conversion is like a second lease of life. God's commandments have become very important to me!"

Toby gave witness: "Medjugorje altered my life completely."

Toby reports candidly on the fears in his soul and his path to faith.

"I come from a village in Bavaria. I grew up with my brother in a Christian family. Every Sunday I had to go to church and often on weekdays too. I had problems with my parents and there were some arguments.

'Increasingly I had the feeling I was not wanted. I was afraid, depressed, reserved and impatient. From a young age, alcohol, nicotine and parties dominated my life. Sometimes I did not want to go on living; everything seemed so meaningless.

'I still went to church every Sunday to please my mother. I had never really understood anything about Holy Mass. Holy Communion was unimportant to me and I only received it at the Church's most important times of year. I did not enjoy doing the work I learnt. I was never really satisfied with my life. I often thought I was a useless person.

'By the time I turned twenty-one I had had a lot of girlfriends and had committed a great many sins. I went to Confession two or three times a year but I was too afraid to mention the more serious sins.

'Luckily I was given the magazine **Medjugorje Currently** by my aunt. Reading of a youth pilgrimage to Medjugorje, I found numerous thoughts went racing through my head. I thought, "My life will have to change; I cannot go on like this!" Finally I decided for this pilgrimage and went there in November 1997.

'I met plenty people and they were joyful and pleasant. I could scarcely believe I was there, where Our Lady is appearing. The longer I stayed there, the more I realized what bad things I had done in my life. Tears of repentance kept coming.

'On the Mount of the Cross I could feel the burden I was constantly carrying round with me. I suddenly felt a longing for Jesus and Mary. I thought, "I would like to take the messages of the Blessed Virgin Mary seriously and live them. My life must change, be renewed and be more orderly and in accordance with Jesus."

'I made a life confession. From then on I began a new life. The Holy Spirit became evident through my joy, security and hope, a feeling of my own worth and my love towards others. In our pilgrim group, everyone helped everyone, as in a family. This pilgrimage altered my life in a fundamental way.

'When I arrived home, I embraced my mother joyfully with tears in my eyes. I said to her, "We must pray the Rosary together today!" Now I would like to hand on this endless love to others. Now I have found out what it means to suffer, fast and make certain sacrifices. Now, also, I have dedicated my life to Mary, convinced she will never abandon me. Trusting in Jesus, I surrender my whole life on this earth to Him. I believe Medjugorje is a little piece of Heaven! I have realized what the most important thing is in my life!"

An unbeliever was converted at the last moment:

At the time of the French Revolution, one of the worst murderers had sworn that no priest would ever enter his house. He was very angry and said he would do any such priest in. Then, when he was lying on his death bed, somebody told a priest that he was ill and dying. The priest rushed to his house to try to save his soul. If the murderer confessed and could repent and be saved, the priest could administer the Sacraments.

When the priest arrived at the door of the man's room, he angrily shouted for a pistol, in order to kill the priest. Nobody gave him a gun and he could not get up himself. Then the man threatened the priest with his fist and told him he had already choked twelve other priests with the same hand.

The priest replied, "That is a falsehood, dear brother. You did not choke twelve, only eleven. I would have been the twelfth one but I am not dead. God kept me alive, to save you from hell. I have come to forgive you and to see that God forgives you too!" The priest then opened his jacket, showed him the scar under his neck and said, "Here are the traces of your hand. Never forget that God is love and pure grace!"

The dying man was speechless and could hardly breathe. That is how godly mercy works. He admitted all his sins, made his peace with God and died in the priest's arms.

A murderer was forgiven by a mother:

There is a street in Bologna called 'Mercy Street' and it is interesting how this street got its name. One day there was a murder in this street, the victim being the only child of a very religious widow who lived here. When the killer realized what he had done, he ran away in fear. He did not know which house the child came from and hid in the house of the child's mother. She, however, did not yet know her child was dead and tried to console the killer. Soon the police brought her dead son back to her.

Despite what had happened, the mother forgave the killer. She thought of the Blessed Virgin Mary, who stood bravely under the cross of her Son and she also thought of Jesus who, dying on the cross, said, "Father, forgive them, for they know not what they do!"

Consider now how far removed we are from Jesus' spirit if we say, "That person has hurt me very much and I cannot forgive him!" How many people there are who, asked during Confession if they are at peace with everyone else, have to answer in the negative! Whoever says he will be good to people who are good to him is speaking like the Pharisees and the tax gatherers of old.

Jesus says we should even love our enemies. He also says, 'If you are not more high-minded than the Pharisees and tax gatherers, you shall not enter into the glory of my Father.' These may seem like harsh words but they are the core of the Gospel. Jesus knew what He was saying. He does not require us to be like God but He does say, 'Be perfect as your Father in Heaven is perfect!' This is meant to guide us to love and forgiveness and away from hate and revenge. Whoever cannot grasp this cannot call himself a follower of Jesus. We are not asked to do what is impossible but to do what is possible with God's help.

This is the Time of Grace

An alcoholic was cured by patience and prayer:

A married woman says, "My husband was an alcoholic, even before we got married. That was a heavy cross for me to carry but I did not leave him because I loved him and wanted to help him. I just prayed I would be able to carry the cross. While praying I repeatedly felt a great power and at times there was a voice within me saying, 'Continue praying, be patient and leave everything to Jesus!'

'For many years now my husband has not touched alcohol. Heaven did hear my prayer. Just before he stopped drinking, I had noticed he had become quite reticent, though he could not talk to me about it. That to me was simply a signal that I should pray even more for him. Finally, on All Saints' Day, I found a letter from him which said, 'I cannot stand this any longer and I am going to do myself in!' Without a word, my husband drove away in the car. I implored all the angels and saints to help. I prayed all that day and night. Then on All Souls' Day he came home, kneeled down and asked me to forgive him, saying, 'My dear wife, forgive me! I don't know what came over me but I wanted to do myself in. I felt an evil force inside me that ordered me to do so. As I was not strong enough to withstand it, I wanted to bow to this pressure. Then, very strongly, I felt something telling me, 'Do not do that! Your wife and all the angels and saints are praying for you!' Then I felt that my heart was much lighter and I asked God to forgive me for wanting to do such a thing.' "

It is worth praying, especially nowadays, this woman concludes. She knows God hears our prayers.

A man called Daniel learned from a dream:

One night, Daniel had a dream of his own death. He considered himself a good, godfearing person. In the dream, he saw in the distance a judge with the Book of Life open. A mysterious force carried him there and also the people with him in his life on earth. Each of them had something to tell the judge.

One said, "This man led me into sin!"

The next one said, "He taught me to lie and cheat!"

Another said, "He taught me to curse and condemn!"

The next one: "I sought small kindnesses from him but did not receive them!"

The next: "He was very selfish!"

The last one: "He was envious, quarrelsome, unfaithful and greedy!"

Then the judge invited him to respond. He said, "It is all true." The judge told him to judge himself and to decide what he deserved. At that moment Daniel broke down. He then woke up in a sweat. The dream, however, helped him so much that he went to see a priest and made a good confession.

St Paul says: "For we must all appear before the judgement seat of Christ, so that each one may receive good or evil, according to what he has done in the body." (2 Cor. 5,10)

Further, he says: "He chose us in Christ before the foundation of the world, that we should be holy and blameless before Him. He destined us in love to be His sons through Jesus Christ, according to the purpose of His will, to the praise of His glorious grace...." (Eph. 1, 4-6)

A family was saved by revering the Most Holy Heart of Jesus:

A poor working man's family were plagued for years by all sorts of woes; yet the mother of the six children saved herself from despair by revering the Most Holy Heart of Jesus. Then, however, she fell ill and the doctor could do nothing more for her. The same day, when her husband came home from the office, he was quite upset, having suddenly lost his job. When he heard his wife's diagnosis as well, he was so shocked that he went into his room and locked the door. After a while he rushed out of the house, leaving behind a letter in which he asked his children to forgive him, because he had decided to take his life. All these blows of fate were simply too much for him to bear.

The oldest son, sensing there was something very wrong with his father, then found the letter and read it. He immediately ran after his father and begged him to go back home with him. The father, however, would not listen. Finally the son took his hand and said, weeping, "Please, Father, there is just one more thing I want to tell you. Have you forgotten that there is a heart so kind and merciful to the sad and the oppressed? We too can be helped by this heart in our hour of great need. This heart calls all those who are tired and burdened, all those in difficulty and despair. Approach this heart and trust in it, Father. I beg of you on behalf of this heart: come back home! Everything will be in accordance with God's will!"

These words touched the father very deeply and freed his soul from despair. "Dear son," he said, with tears in his eyes, "let us go home!" Indeed, the heart of Jesus came to their aid; His grace triumphed! His heart is so good that it always wants to help us. The family were granted a miracle: the mother recovered her health and the father found work again.

After a break of twenty years without the holy Sacraments, the father now began to receive them again. He could no longer live without the grace of Holy Mass, which he recognized as the most valuable thing in life. From then on, he never missed Holy Communion on the first Friday of the month and on every Church holiday of the Blessed Virgin Mary.

A mother recognized her son in a priest she did not know:

A young priest, in Lourdes with his congregation, revealed his secret during a sermon. He said, "Soon after I was ordained to the priesthood, my mother told me she was not my real mother. When I was small, the gypsies had picked me up from somewhere and had then come through her village. They had wanted to blind me, so that I would make a better beggar for them. She had saved me from them with great difficulty. Then I went to school and later became a priest. My foster mother now finally decided to tell me the truth."

When Holy Mass had finished, a woman made her way through the crowd towards the priest. She put her arms round his neck and hugged him. He snapped, "Will you please be sensible and leave me in peace!" The woman would not let go of him, however.

This is the Time of Grace

Tearfully she said to him, "My son, my son, my only son! How long did I search for you in vain? I have found you at last, in the presence of Our Lady. My dear son, the mole on your right hand left me in no doubt."

This is an example for us, too, of how God guides everything that happens. Nothing takes place without His allowing it and without His knowledge! We must simply have total faith in God and seek His will in all things. Then, everything proceeds as God wishes, for our own good and to the greater glory of God.

"A fellow soldier showed me more love than I did him":

After five years on the war front, a soldier returned home, saying war was a school that is indispensable for life. His friends asked him what he had learnt in that school. He said he had learnt there was a man who had shown him more love than he himself had shown.

He explained, "One day he and I were in the same trench, when suddenly a grenade landed between us. What were we to do? It was about to explode and kill both of us within a few seconds. I fainted but he threw himself over the grenade and was blown to pieces. In so doing, he saved me!"

Which of us could do such a thing? For whom would we do it?

Jesus did so for each one of us. He died without sin for us sinners. Let us learn from this. Let us practise it in small ways, so that we are ready for the important things.

Saint Seraphina and Saint Gemma obtained grace for sinners:

St Seraphina once asked of Our Lady that one thousand sinners be converted and she prayed a novena to this end. Then it occurred to her that she had perhaps asked for too much. As she sat lost in thought, Our Lady appeared and said, "Why did you become afraid? Do you think I cannot persuade my Son to have a thousand sinners converted? I can tell you that I have already granted you this wish."

Our Lady took her into Heaven and showed her a great many souls who would have deserved to go to hell, only they were converted and were saved through the intercession and the prayers of the Blessed Virgin.

St Gemma Galgani one day asked the Lord for grace for a sinner. After Gemma had prayed constantly for this, the Saviour recited the worst sins of this sinner, one after the other. Then He refused her request three times. She told Him she would, in that case, appeal to the Saviour's Mother, Mary. He replied that it would then be impossible for Him to refuse to grant her request. An hour later the sinner went to the saint's confessor and humbly confessed all his sins.

Our heavenly Mother's intercession is powerful and her love and mercy are unimaginable.

A story that has the mark of genuine love:

Before the outbreak of civil war, an English girl became engaged to a young man who was then called up to serve in the army. The wedding had to be postponed. The young soldier put great effort into the fighting but he was seriously wounded in a battle.

This is the Time of Grace

His fiancee was waiting for a letter from him and at last one came. It was in someone else's writing and said, "There was some very heavy fighting and I am sorry to tell you I lost both my hands in battle, so that I could not write this myself. I love you as much as before and now even more... and I release you from the responsibility of having promised to marry me."

This letter was never answered. Instead, the girl boarded a train and went to the military hospital. She went looking for the one she loved so much with tears in her eyes. On seeing him, she put her arms round him and kissed him, saying, "I shall never leave you! My hands will take care of you and help you!"

Jean Richepin discovered God's love:

The French poet Richepin wrote a poem entitled 'The Prayer of the Atheists' in which he mocked God, the Church, Jesus and Mary.. He writes roughly as follows: 'I went into a church, kneeled on the cold stone floor, folded my hands and prayed, "God, you do not exist! If you existed, I could never be kneeling before you. By the way, if you are there, send an arrow down from heaven to kill me here on the spot! But you have not sent an arrow and I am still alive. Therefore you cannot exist!" '

If we should wonder why God said nothing to this and whether He could not produce an arrow, the answer is that He is love and mercy. He does not wish to punish people immediately but to be patient with them. In the case of this poet, it was worth waiting, for he was converted and admitted he had made a mistake. He entered the Order of the Trappists, in order to atone; he could also praise God for His patience continually.

A Franciscan monastery has the following custom:

It has long been the custom, in a certain monastery, for one of the monks to go to each person's door after 9 o'clock every evening, knock on it and say, "Brother, please do not forget to say the Lord's Prayer for all those people in the world who are going to sleep tonight with mortal sin in their souls."

Unfortunately there are a great many people nowadays who continue their lives with soul and body in a state of mortal sin. St Thomas was amazed that so many people go to sleep without peace in their soul and in a state of deadly enmity with God.

A Christian should be and live in the grace of God at every moment. If, however, he falls into serious sin, he should immediately repent of it totally and go to Confession as soon as possible.

"I shall tell you how you must sail the stormy sea of the world. Surrender to God and love as a child does, so that his father is fond of him and cannot leave him alone in times of danger." (Therese of Lisieux)

This is the Time of Grace

PART THREE

**"Living means loving
and loving means risking something!"**
(F. Henri Boulad)

**"Let nothing confuse you! Let nothing frighten you!
Everything passes. God does not change.
Patience achieves everything!
Whoever has God lacks nothing!
God alone is sufficient!"**
(Teresa of Avila)

**"Wherever people are enthusiastic
about the matter of Jesus
and are spurred on by it,
there the Holy Spirit is at work!"**
(Norbert Hoffman)

**"The word 'patience'
is a light for the mind and
a fire for the spirit!"**
(Laurence of Brindisi)

The Family as an Inexhaustible Source of Holiness, Love and Life

To speak and write about the family is to speak and write about the first and greatest school of life. The family was and is the most essential and important task in life. It is the basic school of human life, in which each of us develops into a conscientious and responsible person.

The family is the beginning, the source and the root of society, the Church and our homeland. The whole fate of our home, our country and the Church depends on the condition of family life. The essential part of a human being was, is or will be developed in the family. We experience the greatest joys and sadnesses in the bosom of the family. To put it simply: without a good family atmosphere, true and genuine human life would be unthinkable. The sorrows of our life are borne most easily in the family. In the life of the family we also encounter God.

God, who is love, provided us with the family as one of the main tasks in life, as a path of love that leads to God. The creator and founder of the family is God. He provided us with the family as a place of paradise in this vale of tears. God Himself became man in the family at Nazareth. He came to us in order to transform the earth into a paradise and all the people into one big family of God. That is why we are all brothers and sisters in Jesus; we are children of the one heavenly Father. The family is the sanctuary and the hearth of love, an image and likeness of the infinite and infinitely selfless love of God.

The family is like a garden or a greenhouse of life. This is where love creates life; from the family, life flows like an inexhaustible river; here is where body and mind grow. Here a person receives his physical features and his spiritual form. This first and greatest school of life produces saints and criminals, innocent people and sinners, industrious and exemplary people but also thieves and ne'er-do-wells. "As is the family, so too are the community, the Church and the people!" (Dr Ivo Bagaric)

The crisis in the family is a sign of our time:

We are all witnesses of a bitter truth, namely that nowadays everything is in a great and serious crisis. Never has humanity experienced such a serious crisis before. This crisis has especially put the family under attack. So great is the threat or the damage to the family that it is hard to find a remedy. Nearly every second family breaks up. Less and less do we find love, faithfulness, joy, happiness and life in the families, which are being destroyed by unfaithfulness, divorce, abortion, immorality and lack of respect for fertility and the propagation of life.

It is terrible to hear that there are now more than 80 million homeless children on the world's streets. There are numerous children who have become addicted to alcohol or drugs, often the children of divorced parents. Television, newspapers and pornographic material contribute to the disintegration of the family and kill the family atmosphere and its spirit. One may well ask why marriage has become a consumer product. As Dr Ivo Bagaric says, "A man and a woman who really love one another are no longer two inseparable parts of a unit but goods, which one buys, sells, takes, throws away, uses and changes...."

Difficult and fateful times have begun for the family. Bagaric asks, "How can it be that so many men and women love and embrace one another for a short time but then hate one another and argue for a long time, until they separate and start this mad life again with another person? They leave behind only fragments and orphans!" We all know the symptoms: families are unhappy, sick and injured and they break up; the members of the family do not listen to or respect one another any more; each person believes he is the cleverest one. The parents blame the children for everything and the children blame the parents. The older and the younger generation do not understand one another any longer and wage a cold war against one another. This does not solve the problem but only makes it worse.

Where did such a malignant disease, such a crisis and the disintegration of so many families come from and how are they to be explained? This illness and this crisis have been plaguing us for a long time. There are a great many reasons. One of the most common and fateful reasons is that so many families have lost Jesus. He is the basis of a family and He is what keeps it together. The Holy Spirit and willingness to make sacrifices and to be unselfish are what is now lacking in families. The faith is being lost more and more.

This is why the Christian Church is concerned about the state of the family. The Church wants the family to become and to remain a source of holiness, love and life. Pope John Paul II made one year the year of the family for this reason. Many people make the mistake of thinking that a family's good fortune and its future are assured when a lot of money is coming into the household, whether in euros, dollars or whatever. Do we also perhaps think a family's happiness is assured as soon as

This is the Time of Grace

their new furniture is brought into the house? These things can be valuable and useful but they are not sufficient to protect us from disharmony, misery and distress.

The secret of an intact family life is to be found in the worship of God and the obeying of His commandments; this promotes mutual respect and love in all members of the family. If we want to have happy and loyal families, we must bring Christ's message into their midst. This will create such an atmosphere that the true growth of the family can take place.

Happiness in marriage can be attained as follows:

Once the famous statesman Benjamin Franklin was watching some men who were building a house. He particularly noticed one of them, who appeared to be more contented and happier than the others. He went over to him and asked him why. The workman said, "The reason for my happiness is that I have a family worth their weight in gold. No woman I could find anywhere would be a better person than my wife. When I leave the house in the morning to go to work, she kisses me, wishes me God's protection and tells me not to overburden myself or my health during the day. When I go home tired in the evening, she waits at the door for me with the children, greets me with a happy smile and asks me if I am tired. When I go into the house, everything is in order, there is a good dinner waiting, in short, nowhere on earth do I feel as good as at home. I have a family that make me really happy. "

We all know a family that owned nothing, so to speak. They lived in poverty but nowhere on earth was there greater happiness, greater contentment, more peace and more harmony than in that family, the holy family of Nazareth. This family should be the example for all our families.

Everybody must be prepared to make sacrifices. One should accept others and be prepared to help them. Whoever has learnt this will be able to create a genuine family.

The Queen of Peace is calling us:

The Queen of Peace has come amongst us in these difficult and fateful times in order to help us. She is our Mother and she is very worried about saving us. She knows very well that the family is in a great crisis and in great temptation. That is why she tirelessly appeals to the families to pray and appeals to all of us to pray for the families. She really wants God to be the most important one in every family. Only a family which is based and formed on God is a true community of life, love, faithfulness, joy and happiness. God is the foundation and source of family life. Therefore the family should become a sanctuary of life and a source of holiness.

"Dear children! I rejoice because of all of you who are on the way of holiness and I beseech you, by your own testimony help those who do not know how to live in holiness. Therefore, dear children, let your family be a place where holiness is birthed. Help everyone to live in holiness, but especially your own family." (24.7.1986)

The invitation to holiness is meant for everyone. Holiness is lived in the families most easily through an atmosphere of belief and love. The true birthplace of holiness is in fact the family. It is a gift of God.

"Dear children! .... First of all, give your love and example in your families. You say that Christmas is a family feast.

162   This is the Time of Grace

Therefore, dear children, put God in the first place in your families, so that He may give you peace and may protect you not only from war, but also in peace protect you from every satanic attack. When God is with you, you have everything. But when you do not want Him, then you are miserable and lost, and you do not know on whose side you are. Therefore, dear children, decide for God. Then you will get everything." (25.12.1991)

God is the one who has given us this invitation to life. He wants us always to put Him first in our lives. When He is really given this place and does come first, as He deserves, He will give us everything. Our Lady wants us to count on God always. He will give us peace and protect us from Satan's temptations. Our families can only be healed when they return to God completely. Those who have lost all bonds with God are lost souls, pitiable and in a state of wretchedness.

An elderly pilgrim from Italy said, "I am here to thank God for the grace of my conversion. I know I will never be able to thank Him enough. My family had to suffer a lot because of my sinful life. I have returned to God, thanks to the prayer and intercession of the Queen of Peace. Oh, how beautiful it is to live with God and to be happy."

"Dear children! My invitation that you live the messages which I am giving you is a daily one, specially, little children, because I want to draw you closer to the Heart of Jesus. Therefore, little children, I am inviting you today to the prayer of consecration to Jesus, my dear Son, so that each of you may be His. And then I am inviting you to consecration to my Immaculate Heart. I want you to consecrate yourselves as parents, as families and as parishioners so that all belong to God through my heart. Therefore, little children, pray that you comprehend the greatness of this message which I am giving you. I do not want anything for myself, rather all for the salvation of your soul." (25.10.1988)

Here we have the right medicine for all the illnesses that shatter our families. The right answer at the right time is the following: to dedicate ourselves, all families, parishes and everybody, through our prayer, to the Most Holy Heart of Jesus through the Immaculate Heart of Mary personally. This way, everyone belongs to God. We can have God as our friend, as the one who is here to help us.

Everyone is important to God and He has a plan in eternity for each one of us.

"Dear children! Today my invitation is that you pray. Dear children, you are forgetting that you are all important. The elderly are especially important in the family. Urge them to pray. Let all the young people be an example to others by their life and let them witness to Jesus. Dear children, I beseech you, begin to change through prayer and you will know what you need to do." (24.4.1986)

Prayer is what helps us most to bring about a change in our lives. This is why Our Lady tirelessly recommends prayer. "Dear children! Today I wish to call you to pray, pray, pray! In prayer you will perceive the greatest joy and the way out of every situation that has no exit. Thank you for starting up prayer. Each individual is dear to my heart. And I thank all who have encouraged their families to pray." (28.3.1985)

"Dear children! I beseech you to start changing your life in the family. Let the family be a harmonious flower that I wish to give to Jesus. Dear children, let every family be active in prayer for I wish that the fruits in the family be

164   This is the Time of Grace

seen one day. Only that way shall I give you all, like petals, as a gift to Jesus in fulfilment of God's plans." (1.5.1986)

"Dear children! Today I call you to renew prayer in your families. Dear children, encourage the very young to prayer and the children to go to Holy Mass." (7.3.1985)

"Dear children! Today is the day on which I give you the message for the parish but not everyone in the parish accepts the message and lives it. I am saddened and I want you to listen to me, dear children, and to live my messages. Every family must pray and also read the Bible!" (14.2.1985)

This is the only message to date in which Our Lady requires something of us. Indeed, every family that wants to grow spiritually must pray as a family and read the Bible. That is the spiritual nourishment without which the family cannot live. There are many families which are endangered just because they cannot pray, maybe owing to lack of time. All the families that are destroyed have surely not prayed properly.

Numerous times Our Lady has appealed to the families to fast and pray for peace.

"Dear children! Today I invite you to pray for peace. At this time peace is being threatened in a special way, and I am seeking from you to renew fasting and prayer in your families. Dear children, I desire you to grasp the seriousness of the situation and that much of what will happen depends on your prayers. You are praying only a little. Dear children, I am with you and I am inviting you to begin to pray and fast seriously as in the first days of my coming." (25.7.1991)

"Dear children! Today I call you to the renewal of prayer in your homes. The work in the fields is over; now devote yourselves to prayer. Let prayer take the first place in your families." (1.11.1984)

Let us not forget: "When the Lord decided to save humanity and make it holy, He started at its base, the family. He Himself was born into such a family bringing holiness into it, though not only into this one family but also into any family, right to the last one. He chose the holy family of Nazareth to be an example, an ideal, for any human family. He also grants us His help, strength and grace, so that any family can attain and realize this example. As far as married people are concerned, when the Lord is the basis and focal point of their life and love, they will win through, they will deepen their life together and extend it, even when there are not only flowers and songs around them." (Dr Ivo Bagaric)

The famous French author Rene Bazin wrote to his fiancee, "Pray to God that He be with us! That is the source, the strength and the goal of our love!" Here we have the right prescription and the right advice for any family!

Saint Paul says: 'Put on then compassion, kindness, lowliness, meekness and patience...' (Col. 3, 12) Without these virtues, there are no fortunate and joyous families. Be unselfish and accept the others lovingly; endure patiently their mistakes and shortcomings. This is necessary for anyone who wants to grow in the virtues.

Tireless and ardent prayer converts the family:

A harmonious family, or so everyone thought, lived in a town on the bank of a river. One day Grandfather Stanko said, "Robert, my child, tomorrow is Sunday; do you want

This is the Time of Grace

to go to church with Grandpa? There will be a lot of children there."

"What, church? What nonsense are you talking, you silly old man?" screamed his daughter Zorica angrily. "If you want to go, then go, but why do you ask it of the child? Anyhow, tomorrow there is a football match on, which Robert would like to watch."

Robert, aged seven, said, "Mother, I would like to go to church with Grandpa for once!"

"You're going to the football match, and that's all there is about it!" shouted Grandpa's son-in-law Vlado.

Such arguments went on day by day and year by year. Grandfather Stanko went to his room every evening, kneeled in front of the picture of Our Lady, where there was always a lighted candle, and prayed, "Almighty God! You, who see and know everything, convert my lost family! Lead them the right way, the way of faith!"

The grandfather prayed and Zorica, Vlado and Robert went to nightclubs or listened to blaring music at home, to which they danced rock'n'roll. Then came the day on which Grandfather Stanko had to leave this world for ever. His family gave him a simple burial, without a ceremony.

The family continued their way of life after Grandfather died. Robert was now in seventh class at school. One day he went into his grandfather's room. He wanted to clear out all the old things and throw them away, to set up a disco there. He threw everything out of the door. Finally he came to the picture of Our Lady, ripped it down and was about to throw it out with the other things. Suddenly he saw a piece of paper in the picture frame. Taking it out, he read: "Robert, as long as I live I will pray for you and for your conversion from your life of sin! I will do so here in this room in front of this picture and when I die I will pray in Heaven for you!"

These words, written in his grandfather's trembling hand, worked a miracle in the boy. Coming out of the room, he was pale, quiet and downcast, a different boy from when he went in. From that day on, he went another way from that of his parents, as they were leading him into sin and into company which uttered blasphemies. He invented excuses, saying he had to study. He obtained a Bible and read it; he learnt the Lord's Prayer and numerous other prayers. His parents knew nothing of this; if they had, they would have immediately tried to put a stop to it, before he had really set out on the path to Jesus.

Robert finished eighth class. Then he bravely told his mother he was going to study to become a priest. His mother screamed, "What? Anything else you like, but not that! No!"

Robert became a priest despite this; so at his first Holy Mass his parents sat proudly by their son. Now they have recently begun to go to church on Sundays and worship God piously.

When Robert solemnly raised the host at his first Holy Mass, he heard the voice of his grandfather say, "God has granted me the grace of your own conversion, my dear grandson; and He has given you the grace, too, of your parents' conversion through you. Now my prayer has been heard and my family are on the right path. Oh my Lord God Almighty!"

The following are suggestions on how to bring up children well:

Bear in mind that a child is a gift from God. This is the greatest blessing of all. Each child is an individual in his own right and we must allow him to be what he is.

Do not mortify his spirit when he makes a mistake. Never compare him with others who are better than your child in some way.

Understand that anger and discontent are natural feelings. Help your child to express these feelings in some acceptable way, so that they are not suppressed into his subconscious mind, only to resurface later in the form of psychological and physical illnesses.

Be sensible and consistent in the upbringing of the child. Do not let yourself be swayed by anger. A punishment must correspond to the misdemeanour and not be greater.

Never side with the child against your spouse. The child would then be in an emotional conflict and he would feel guilt, bias and uncertainty.

Do not pander to every little wish he has but do reward the child when he deserves it. Do not threaten the child with things you would not carry out. Do not promise the child anything without fulfilling your promise. A child that loses faith in his own parents can scarcely have faith in anyone again.

Do not smother the child with superficial love. True and genuine love is seen in daily life. Teach the child to love others and to love God above all else.

Teach the child the value of work. A useful life is one of happiness and fulfilment. A life of pleasure only and of searching for one's own satisfaction is valueless and meaningless.

Do not simply send the child to church but take him there yourself. Children learn by example. This applies when you show him and also when you tell him something. If you plant the seed of profound faith in God, it will give him help and strength, even if everything else should disappoint him.

(Check this advice yourself! Perhaps it will help you, too, in bringing up your child optimally!)

He will be grateful to you and God will reward you! (quoted from Kana, 2, 1980)

A girl named Christina wrote a shattering letter:

"Dear Father,

You are the only one in this world who understood me. I am writing to you for the last time, as I have no opportunity left to talk to you personally. I know you love me very much, Father.

I know that what I have decided to do will be terrible for you. You know just how unhappy I am, though. My unhappiness began with the tragedy that took place in my youth. My lost virginity was the beginning of my ruin. I shall suffer as long as I live.

170

I shall not live much longer, for I am going to end my life. My soul is bleeding and my heart is breaking with pain. I cannot live alone. There is no-one who can make me happy. They all only want my body and when they get it they leave me.

Dear Father, I am not strong enough to live in purity as I once did and so I am very, very unhappy. Do not cry too much. I was not worthy of you.

Love,

Christina"

This was a girl from the country who went to the city to study. Her morals deteriorated here. She could not live with her bad conscience. One must admit that there was something profound and valuable in this soul. She was truly looking for genuine love, even through her fall. The lesson to be learned is eternally true: sex is not love.

The Holy Spirit

Source of Consolation and Counsel

We are all more or less witnesses to a fact that cannot be denied: there is a great crisis everywhere. Humanity has never been in such danger as now. Uncertainty, fear, distress and despair are our constant companions. We are all threatened by incurable diseases like cancer and AIDS. Violence is on the increase. Drugs are spreading like the plague. There are numerous natural catastrophes. The number of crisis areas in the world now exceeds eighty.

The constant struggle between good and evil is not decreasing but is even intensifying daily. Humanity is trying to find a way out of this serious situation. Man, a free and rational being, is longing for a meaningful life and true joy and happiness.

In the Acts of the Apostles, we read something very relevant to our time too. When Paul reached Ephesus, he looked for the disciples of Jesus and asked them, "Did you receive the Holy Spirit when you believed?" They said, "No, we have never even heard that there is a Holy Spirit." (Acts 19, 1-2)

If we were to ask numerous Christians the same question today, we might well be given the same answer. They may know that there is a Holy Spirit but that is all they know on the subject. Many know neither what being this is nor what this being means in their lives; they also do not know what part the Holy Spirit plays in the life of a practising believer and in the Church itself.

One must admit that there are many people today who live and act as if the Holy Spirit and Its influence did not

This is the Time of Grace

exist. We should not forget, however, that the Holy Spirit is effective in the Church of today just as It was in the early Church. It is also effective in every believing soul.

Who is the Holy Spirit?

The Holy Spirit is the third person of the Most Holy Trinity, being true God with the Father and the Son. It is eternal, unfathomable, all-powerful; Creator and Lord of all created, as are the Father and the Son. The Holy Spirit comes from the Father and the Son, through their identical will and through their love, as from a single source. The Father engenders the Son from eternity and similarly from eternity the Holy Spirit is sent out by the Father and the Son.

If holiness develops, the process involved is attributed in particular to the Holy Spirit. It causes souls to become holier. The Holy Spirit is the love of the Father and the Son. It is the gift of the Father to the Son and also the gift of the Son to the Father. Again, It is the gift of the Father and the Son to the Church.

The Holy Spirit is present in many ways. It is the spiritual presence of resurrected Jesus in the Church. It is a presence in the form of Jesus at a time in the world's history. This presence is nevertheless a person, in a mysterious way, namely the third person of the Most Holy Trinity. It is the soul of the Church. Without the Holy Spirit, God would be far away; Christ would be a figure in history; the Gospel would be writings dead and buried.

Without the Holy Spirit, the Church can be nothing but an institution; its authority only domination; its mission just propaganda; the cult merely a challenge; Christian behaviour only the morality of prisoners. As it is, however, everything is enfolded in the Holy Spirit and the world is longing for the Kingdom of Heaven. Jesus, resurrected, is present; the Gospel is life's strength; the Church is threefold mutuality; the authority is serving that frees us; the mission is Pentecost; a church-service is an act of remembrance and also anticipation; people's behaviour gives them a likeness to God (as Ignatius says).

The Holy Spirit is an undeserved gift, a grace that is among us (cf. Rom. 8,11; 1 Cor. 3,16). It is a good heavenly guest in our soul. Our body is Its temple (cf. 1 Cor. 6,19). It makes us into a new being, into an image of God. Its influence makes us similar to Christ (Rom. 8,29) and perfect people of God. It renews the face of the earth (cf. Ps. 104,30).

The Holy Spirit is our first and chief spiritual guide. It is not possible to imagine a perfect spiritual life without the Holy Spirit. It teaches us, advises us, warns us, consoles us and guides us. It does this through, for example, a priest, a person devoted to God, one's parents, the Holy Bible, a worthwhile book or one's own conscience. The Holy Spirit helps us to bear our cross patiently, to overcome temptations and to fulfil one's Christian duties conscientiously.

Everything that spurs us on towards what is good, motivated by love of God, comes from the Holy Spirit. 'All who are led by the Spirit of God are sons of God.' (Rom. 8,14) The Holy Spirit, making us similar to Christ, unites us with Itself; anyone who does not have the Spirit of Christ cannot be part of the Holy Spirit. (Rom. 8,9) The Holy Spirit teaches us to pray as we should. (Rom. 8,26) Nobody can say "Jesus is Lord" except by the Holy Spirit. (1 Cor. 12,3) It brings truth, peace and joy. (Acts 13,52; Rom. 14,17; John 14,17; John 16,13)

This is the Time of Grace

The wish to give oneself to others and to be with them is a wish that is love. God's love is one that creates and one that attracts us to Him. The power of the Holy Spirit is present here. Where, on the other hand, there is hatred, sin or disunity, the Holy Spirit cannot be present; It cannot enter such a place. Reconciliation is what opens the way to the Holy Spirit and Jesus Christ is the one who always brings reconciliation, peace and forgiveness. We can only receive the Holy Spirit when we are reconciled with God and other people, as Jesus recommends.

The Holy Spirit is always waiting discreetly, ready and glad to help any believer in any of life's situations. It would like to heal us and save us. If ever we forget this Spirit or reject It; if we ignore It or fail to ask It for help, then we are alone in the face of failure, powerlessness, despair and defeat. We may give way to the temptation of complaining about God and about the situation we are in.

We should never forget that the Holy Spirit changes us inwardly, though never without us. We are called upon to work together with It and to surrender to Its guidance and obey its wisdom. It is a sin to offer resistance when it is at work. Moreover, as St Paul says, one should not quench the Spirit and limit its effectiveness. (1 Thess. 5, 19)

The Holy Spirit in the history of the renewal of the world:

The Holy Spirit is continually at work. It is what makes us holy and nearer perfection. It guides everything and rules over everything. Without Its influence and intervention, we cannot understand God's plan of renewal and its realization. The Church fathers, especially those of Greece, demonstrate this very clearly and emphasize it.

Saint Basil joyfully writes, "Do you think about the creation? It was accomplished in the Holy Spirit, which
strengthened it and made the heavens lovelier. Do you
think about Jesus Christ's coming into the world? The
Holy Spirit prepared it and, when the time had come,
Mary was imbued with the Holy Spirit, so that the coming
of Jesus was realized. Do you think about the foundation
of the Church? It is the achievement of the Holy Spirit.
Do you think about Christ's return? The Holy Spirit will be
present then too, when the dead are resurrected from the
graves and when our Saviour from Heaven appears." (St
Basil, 'The Holy Spirit', pp. 16 and 19)

The Holy Spirit brings everything to life, unites everything
and sets everything moving. It is the spring of water,
welling up to eternal life. (cf. John 4, 14) The Father,
through the Holy Spirit, revives people who were dead
through sin; their bodies too will be given life. (cf. Rom. 8,
10-11)

The Holy Spirit renews believers through Baptism.
Through the Sacrament of Confirmation, It strengthens
them, so that they spread and defend the faith in word
and deed as true witnesses of Christ. (Lumen Gentium) If
they are persecuted, It will speak through their lips. (Matt.
10, 20) It guides the Church into total truth. (John 16, 13)
It keeps the Church young by means of the Gospel.
Guided by the Holy Spirit, the Church observes the faith
with care and interprets it in truth. (Lumen Gentium)
God's love is poured into our hearts through the Holy
Spirit. (Rom. 5, 5)

Through the Sacraments and Its ministry, the Holy Spirit
guides the people who belong to God and makes them
holy; It embellishes them with the virtues. It enriches our
soul with Its gifts. It spurs us on to lead a virtuous life and

This is the Time of Grace

turns us away from evil. It prays in us and bears witness to our being sons of God. (Gal. 4, 6) We should not suppress Its voice by succumbing to the desires of the flesh or by occupying ourselves with unworthy things. (cf. 1 Thess. 4, 3-8, 10-11; 5, 6)

It is important to remember nowadays that Jesus Christ and the Holy Spirit both play a part in the renewal of the world. Jesus is the wisdom of God. The Holy Spirit is the power of God. Jesus was conceived through the power of the Holy Spirit. After His Baptism, fasting and being tempted, Jesus preached and did the works of God, steeped in the Holy Spirit. He prayed and rejoiced in the Spirit of Holiness. He promised the apostles the Holy Spirit and sent It out from the Father, for It to complete His work and all works of holiness. (Fourth Eucharistic Prayer) It is the Holy Spirit that inspired the prophets and that has led the Church all the way into our era. (cf. Dr. T. Ivancic, 'Encountering the Living God', p. 93)

In the Old Testament, the Holy Spirit is the power and the force with which God performed wondrous deeds in the creation, thus preparing its renewal. In the New Testament, what is new about the Holy Spirit is that It is a spirit of salvation and renewal. It is the power of God's love for the world. In the power of the Holy Spirit, Jesus was embodied in human form and brought salvation to the world. It is a spirit that is thus the Spirit of Christ. This does not mean It is only sent out by Jesus; It is always the Spirit of both the Son and the Father. What is meant is that, with Jesus' death on the cross, the Holy Spirit comes to us in a new way.

The true influence of the Holy Spirit:

A contemporary theologist describes the influence of the Holy Spirit as follows: "The Spirit that Christ promised to send to His disciples, which is also His own Spirit, is what enables the Gospel to send roots down to the very depths of the soul. The same Spirit is able to disseminate the Gospel all over the world. It digs new depths in a person and thereby makes him similar to the 'depths of God'. It draws him out of himself and sends him to the farthest reaches of the earth. It makes him into a being capable of living a communal life. It forms both the individual and the community." (Henry de Lubac)

The Holy Scriptures clearly tell us that the Holy Spirit is at work both inwardly and invisibly and also outwardly and visibly. It is there to protect us (cf. John 15, 26); to guide us to complete truth (cf. John 16, 13); to teach us and remind us of what Jesus promised us (cf. John 16, 15). The Holy Spirit speaks of future events. (cf. John 16, 13) It is what joins with our own spirit when we call 'Abba!' to the Heavenly Father. (cf. Rom. 8, 15) It lends us Its gifts and what is useful to us. (cf. 1 Cor. 12, 8-10 and Gal. 5, 22) It dwells in us. (Rom. 5, 5) It is what helps us to pray. (Rom. 8, 26) It makes the world holy and makes of us Its temple. Through It we live and we can perform miracles and effect healings. (cf. Gal. 3, 5 and Acts 4, 30) It opens the hearts of people and makes us witnesses of Jesus. It is the soul of the Church. It gathers us all together and fills us with the spirit of love. Through Jesus, we have access to the Father in the Holy Spirit.

The Holy Spirit works in various ways. The history of the Church shows this clearly. We are assured of it by the saints, by different Church communities and by various movements in the Church. In the 'Acts of the Apostles'

178   This is the Time of Grace

we read that the first followers of Jesus were gathered together in prayer and brotherly love when, all at once, they were filled with the Holy Spirit. (cf. Acts 2, 4) They were baptised with the Holy Spirit, in order to be His witnesses to the ends of the earth. Thus, the mighty source of consolation and counsel transformed this small, fearful community into a living, courageous Church, to be witnesses of Jesus and of His being the resurrection and the Life. Jesus had told them ahead that they would be given power by the Holy Spirit. (cf. Acts 1, 5 and 8)

The Holy Spirit is meant for all of us, for the whole Church and for each of us in the Church. When Jesus says, 'Peace be with you!' and 'Receive the Holy Spirit!' (John 20, 21), He is addressing all of us too, who were born later. Pentecost continues and we should keep it alive in us. The Holy Spirit wishes to give us Its help and strength, so that we develop into genuine Christians filled with holiness. The Spirit is what helps us grow in virtues of all kinds. This is why we should ask It to grant us the grace of becoming living proof of Jesus Christ. We have been sealed with the Holy Spirit for the day of redemption and therefore we ought not to disappoint or grieve this Spirit. (cf. Eph. 4, 30) It is even more important not to sin against the Holy Spirit!

Gifts from the Holy Spirit which change people:

Jesus sent the Holy Spirit to stay with us always. He said It is our counsel and will remain so. This means It is like a lawyer for us, who defends us against evil and wickedness in the world. The Holy Spirit will console us, guide us and encourage us. It will be a witness of everything with us and in us.

The Holy Spirit is the mighty force that changes us believers, making us into new people and friends of God. It renews everything and brings us truth, justice and peace. It alters a person as an individual and gives him light; he can then see the value of the Church and begin a life of fulfilment in God. He understands the Word of God and thirsts for prayer and the Sacraments, which yield fruit. The Holy Spirit also grants him Its own special gifts, so that the influence of God on him becomes quite apparent. It gives him the fruits of love, peace, joy, kindness, wisdom, gentleness, faithfulness, sobriety, humility, charity, justice, courage, determination, temperance and a great many others. These virtues enable the believer to ward off sin and to overcome evil in himself and in the world. This makes for a better society.

The powerful influence of the Holy Spirit is evident nowadays in various movements within the Church. The charismatic movement is particularly strong and its members are new witnesses of Jesus. Today it is possible to speak in 'new languages' (cf. 1 Cor. 14); there are individuals and prayer groups in the Church healing illnesses and infirmities; certain people have the gift of prophecy; there is a new spirit of evangelizing with the power of God; people are being freed of evil forces; there are people with powers that were evident in the early Church.

The Holy Spirit has the special power of enabling prayers to change the world and individual people in our world. When we pray to the Holy Spirit and ask It to be with us, then It can renew the individual and similarly society, destroying what is not good; It needs people through whom It can act. A believer who loves God and forgives his enemies is someone who enables the Holy Spirit to change an enemy into a friend. This way, where there

This is the Time of Grace

was disharmony between people or even war, the Holy Spirit brings about a change for the better and finally peace. God needs people who pray!

How to experience the Holy Spirit:

The first requirement for experiencing the Holy Spirit is to wish for It and Its virtues. Then we should read the New Testament and remember the parts in which the Spirit is promised to us. Then we should turn to God and let Him take first place in our lives. We should repent of all our sins and renounce everything that is at variance with God and His will. Then it is time to start praying steadfastly that we may be given the grace of experiencing the Holy Spirit; we should pray for this for at least twenty minutes daily. The darkness will begin to disappear and what is not good in us will be overcome more and more. In their place will come a new realisation of the reality of God, both in our mind and in our heart. We will feel that a wonderful new life is beginning. We are advised to persevere in such prayers, sensibly and sincerely; finally we shall feel that God is near us and that faith is precious to us. It is very valuable to pray together with someone who shares our convictions.

In this way, we experience that prayer becomes a talk with our God. Our goal, the Spirit of God, becomes more accessible. We feel more peaceful, healthier, happier and more normal. We work better and make better use of our leisure time. Even the people around us change; as Pope John Paul II said, where people are praying, the Holy Spirit is at work. We discover the world of God and the Spirit and we are delighted at finding this pearl. Now we can grow. We should pray and allow God to show His power through us and our work. We should work with love in our heart. A joyous, fulfilled life is totally within reach. The saints are just normal people who have taken this step and then continued.

The Holy Spirit wishes to accompany us, guide and teach us, take us much nearer to the Father and Jesus, enable us to play a new role in the world and help us to pray in joy and to live a life of joy. Let us be open to the love that God is offering us. If a member of a prayer group has received the gifts of the Holy Spirit, it suffices that he pray for those who would like to receive them. The possibility was given them through their Baptism and Confirmation. The Holy Spirit can be experienced by means of conversion and then prayer with great faith. They will be able to experience the Spirit and Its gifts once these cease to be latent and become activated.

We are living in unusual times, times of grace; they are sometimes called the last times, when God is manifestly at work, as His miraculous signs show us. A great many people, however, do not receive the graces God is sending us. The reason may be that nobody has told them of what God is offering us and wants to give us. Prayer and giving witness are what will help them find God and receive His graces. (cf. Dr T. Ivancic)

The greatest signs of the influence of the Holy Spirit are conversion and trust in God. To entrust oneself to God is something most people find difficult and only grace can show the way and give a person sufficient faith to realize this. The apostles prayed together steadfastly and then they received the Holy Spirit. (cf. Acts 1, 14)

We read (Acts 2, 1-4): "When the day of Pentecost had come, they were all together in one place. Suddenly a sound came from Heaven like the rush of a mighty wind and it filled all the house where they were sitting. And there appeared to them tongues as of fire, distributed

182

and resting on each one of them. They were all filled with the Holy Spirit and began to speak in other tongues, as the Spirit gave them utterance."

Jesus said, "Unless one is born anew, he cannot see the Kingdom of God." (John 3, 3) and "Unless one is born of water and the Spirit, he cannot enter the Kingdom of God." (John 3, 5)

To be born anew means the following:
We believe God makes everything possible so that we can be born anew.
We decide to free ourselves of all obstacles, ties and errors.
We make ourselves open to the Holy Spirit and accept It.
We decide to be similar to Jesus.
We do, think, feel and speak only what is in accordance with God's will.

Love, the greatest gift of the Holy Spirit:

Through love, we make others happy and we are made happy too. It is the greatest gift of the Holy Spirit and all Its other gifts are more or less included in love.

We should love others, without exception and without making differences between other people. If we have a problem with someone, we must start to love this person. We should find a way and a situation to let this person become aware of our love. We will soon have a friend in such a person.

Someone gave witness of Jesus' love for us as follows: "I became really happy for the first time when I realized that You, Lord, are my greatest love!"

Qualities of the Spirit of Love:

Joy is the fruit of love.
Peace is the security of love.
Kindness is the warmth of love.
Friendship is the sharing of love.
Patience is the endurance of love.
Gentleness is the humility of love.
Forgiveness is the mercy of love.
Faithfulness is the reliability of love.
Moderation is the victory of love.

The Queen of Peace invites us to become open to the influence of the Holy Spirit:

"Dear children! These days I call you especially to open your hearts to the Holy Spirit. Especially during these days the Holy Spirit is working through you. Open your hearts and surrender your life to Jesus so that He works through your hearts and strengthens you in faith..." (23.5.1985)

"Dear children! You are absorbed with material things, but in the material you lose everything that God wishes to give you. I call you, dear children, to pray for the gifts of the Holy Spirit which are necessary for you now in order to be able to give witness to my presence here and to all that I am giving you. Dear children, let go to me so I can lead you completely. Don't be absorbed with material things...." (17.4.1986)

"Dear children! No, you do not know how many graces God is giving you. You do not want to move ahead during these days when the Holy Spirit is working in a special way. Your hearts are turned toward things of the earth and they preoccupy you. Turn your hearts toward

This is the Time of Grace

prayer and seek the Holy Spirit to be poured out on you..." (9.5.1985)

"Dear children! Tomorrow night, pray for the Spirit of Truth, especially you of the parish. You need the Spirit of Truth to be able to convey the messages just the way they are, neither adding anything to them, nor taking anything away from them, but just the way I said them. Pray for the Holy Spirit to inspire you with the spirit of prayer, so you will pray more. I, your Mother, tell you that you are praying little." (9.6.1984)

"Dear children! Today I wish to say to everyone in the parish to pray in a special way to the Holy Spirit for enlightenment. From today God wishes to test the parish in a special way in order that He might strengthen it in faith..." (11.4.1985)

"Dear children! You are not conscious of the messages which God is sending you through me. He is giving you great graces but you do not comprehend them. Pray for enlightenment! If you only knew how great are the graces God is granting you, you would be praying without ceasing!" (8.11.1984)

We have seen that Jesus (the second person in the Most Holy Trinity) sent us the Holy Spirit (the third person in the Most Holy Trinity). The Holy Spirit being, in turn, the power of God (the first person in the Most Holy Trinity), it would be appropriate to end with this tribute to God, the Father of all things.

The universe is the genius of God.
The creation is the majesty of God.
All life is the masterpiece of God.
The light is the splendour of God.
The Spirit is the power of God.
Lord Jesus is the wisdom of God.
The Gospel is the truth of God.
Our Lady is the art of God.
Paradise is the eternity of God.
God is; God is holy; God is love.

This is the Time of Grace

Is There a Paradise and a Hell?

The well-known American bishop, Fulton Sheen, tells an old story which, for us too, could be instructive and meaningful. It goes as follows. After a priest had preached enthusiastically about Paradise, he asked the members of his congregation to stand if they would like to go to Paradise. Everyone stood up, except for a man in the front row who firmly remained seated. Somewhat surprised, the priest asked them all to sit down and for anyone to stand who wanted to go to hell. Nobody stood up. That man at the front was still sitting, so the priest asked him curiously to tell him where he wanted to go. The man answered, "Me? I would like to stay sitting here always."

It would be neither useful nor clever to live without any cares, but just to eat, drink, smoke, enjoy life and stay unperturbed, without bothering about the big questions and problems of life or the eternal values of our existence. Is there a Heaven (Paradise) and a hell? Some say it is naive to believe this and laughable to think about it. Others say they are not interested in such things. Is this possible? Maybe one lives more calmly if one never thinks about life. This, however, is only the bliss of an intoxicated person who has silenced his conscience by force. Those who deny the existence of hell are not sure of their assertion or of the ideas they nurture and use to comfort themselves. How do they know that Paradise and hell are only illusions or just stories for children?

There is an old saying that nobody has ever come back from beyond to tell us there are such things. That is scarcely any help, however, for it is also true that nobody has ever come back to assure us we need not worry because there is nothing after death. Besides, even if some-body had come back, who would have believed him? He would quickly have been silenced for upsetting the peace. There is one person, however, who came back and who could not be forgotten or made to vanish. He revealed everything to us, precisely, clearly, truthfully and impressively! This must be confronted, especially nowadays.

In the history of humanity, there are numerous instances in which God has allowed people to appear in this vale of tears, in order to indicate a great truth to us, namely that life continues in eternity. Is there a Paradise and a hell? What a question! I couldn't care! I don't even want to think about it! So what if they exist? This question is not an-swered by simply rejecting it. To care about it is vital! It concerns our eternity: a joyous one or a terrible one!

Everyone is more or less   interested in what is behind the mysterious reality of the grave. We want to find out more about what will happen to us after death. Everyone   feels more or less that our existence will go on. Our soul has a notion of this reality. The idea we have of it, however, is not necessarily right.

Only Jesus Christ has given us light and certainty, for He lived, died, was awakened to life again and was resur-rected. He shed light on the great mysteries of life through His godly authority, which cannot deceive us.

The resurrection of Jesus Christ is an absolute fact. What did He want to show us or confirm through it? He showed us that He is true God and true Man, that His teachings are truthful and that we will also be resurrected one day. That means there is life after death, not only life of the soul but also life of the body. After His resurrection, He appeared to the disciples with His real and genuine body. They saw Him and touched Him. He even ate food with

188   This is the Time of Grace

them. His body was, however, different; namely, it was shining with splendour and vitality. It was a body immune to all obstacles, weaknesses, illnesses and tiredness. It was immortal and not subject to decay, being the same yesterday, today and tomorrow.

Jesus thus revealed to us three truths that are beyond the grave, first through what He told us and secondly through what He did after His death. These are:

Every person will be resurrected!
Every person will be judged!
Every person will go either to Paradise or to hell!

Some people find it difficult to believe these things revealed to us by Jesus and so they object to them. They are supposed to be impossible and incomprehensible and therefore unacceptable. Is one right to think like this? With the naked eye one cannot discern objects that are far away, without using optical aids. If one has a telescope, one can see farther. Believing is the telescope of our soul. It is the light that illuminates the darkness of the grave and of death. The condition, however, is that one must trust in Jesus, the Son of God (i.e. believe Him). Whoever is not capable of this cannot believe anybody, not even himself.

It is true that life after death is and will always be a mystery. It is something that surpasses all the laws of space and time. That is why it is so hard to understand it all. When a person lets God's grace be active in him, he no longer finds it hard to grasp these things and to accept them as reality.

In the Gospel, the dreadful day of judgement is portrayed vividly. Our Lord will come in splendour, to judge solemnly the whole of mankind. After everybody has been resurrected, each one will be designated his place: some to the right-hand side, some to the left. "Come, 0 blessed of my Father; inherit the Kingdom prepared for you from the foundation of the world." (Matt. 25, 34) "Then He will say to those at His left hand, 'Depart from Me, you cursed, into the eternal fire prepared for the devil and his angels.' " (Matt. 25, 41)

Some people find this too simple. Why? Whatever they say, Jesus was not naive in the slightest. He knew exactly what He was saying. What did He say in the Gospel that did not take place? He speaks very clearly. He does not speak jokingly! We should not forget that.

It must be quite clear, even to us humans with our limited mind, that good souls cannot spend eternity with murderers, immoral people, those who practise sorcery or worship vain idols or those who are liars; nor could or should God spend eternity with such souls.

Some people may think Jesus will carry out this fateful division of the souls in an arbitrary manner. Therefore they do not think it is acceptable. These people should realize that God gave us free will; as long as we are living in this world, we can choose freely. Each of us can decide for good or evil, for God or against God. Depending on which way we decide, we can either promote goodness, truth and love in ourselves or we can destroy them if we want the opposite. In so doing, we decide ourselves for Heaven or for hell. On the last day, Jesus will merely bring to light the godly or the demonic qualities of each individual. These two natures are opposites and cannot share the same destiny. That day will bring a sublime and wonderful demonstration of the justice and the love of God! It is not easy to imagine that day but it is easy to believe in it, for Jesus said it will come and He never makes a mistake; He is beyond error through His divine nature.

Let us observe some of the truths spoken by Jesus. He predicted His death at a certain time and His resurrection. They both took place as predicted, even though there had been scepticism among His followers. He was seen by many people in many places after His resurrection, as must be admitted by those who have tried to explain it away. He foretold the persecution of His followers and it also took place. He foretold the destruction of the temple of Jerusalem and this also occurred. Even the greatest of sceptics cannot take the statements of Jesus lightly.

The Lord said, "Heaven and earth will pass away but My words will not." This means the day of the Last Judgement will come. Not even the angels know when it will be. On that day, Jesus will solemnly declare who among us have deserved a reward and who a punishment. While the Lord was living on earth, He told the parable of the rich man and poor Lazarus, the former going to the underworld and the latter to Abraham's bosom after death. By this, Jesus did not mean that all poor people go to Paradise and all rich people go to hell. He was simply showing us that, after we die, there are two different realities and therefore two unalterable destinies for our time in eternity.

To make it clear: God did not create hell. Hell is the consequence of sin. Hell was created by fallen angels, led by Lucifer, through their arrogance and disobedience. Hell is a state caused by the sinner himself through the perpetual rejection of God and His love and the constant consumption of the poison of sin. It is similar to an alcoholic who ruins himself in many ways through his unhealthy way of life. Hell means the definitive ruin of what is godly in a person. Though created for truth and love, someone who has embraced untruth and hatred has poisoned what was godly in his soul. Hell is a consequence of the misuse of human free will and freedom. The existence of the state of hell does not mean that God is any less good or merciful. He has even shown His infinite mercy to precisely those who want to reject Him. Those who reject God create hell in this way and so they want it to exist. God died on the cross for the very purpose of saving all of humanity from sin and its consequence, hell; God's sacrifice on the cross also opened the door to Paradise for those worthy of it. Sin is what is unworthy of people, created to be God's children. The existence of hell is often denied precisely by those who bring it into being by their own sinful behaviour.

Jesus made every effort to convince us that life, love and joy are to be found in God. He would like to give all of this to humanity. Without Him, there is no blessedness for mankind. As long as one still has one's body and one's earthly life, one may fail to see this, unfortunately. One may not even be convinced of it but be lost in the superficial joys of the world and in apparent happiness, although one's conscience is aware of the terrible error one is making. After one dies, all errors disappear; every condemned person will recognize that God is the only source of joy and our only permanent bliss.

We all long for true happiness. The fulfilment of all human longings and aspirations is in our God. Sin is the obstacle to finding God and being with Him in the true peace and joy that only He can give. He loves us and we should simply return that love. Every person ought to think what awaits him if he rejects grace, which is God Himself. That person is lost and ruined for ever. How terrible this is! Jesus Himself told us of these dreadful consequences; for Judas, the traitor, it would have been better never even to

This is the Time of Grace

have existed. The life of Jesus was a triumph and a life of ultimate love; the life of Judas was the opposite.

Jesus helped us to understand His thoughts by illustrating them through parables. He spoke of the weeds among the wheat. The wheat is taken into the barn; the weeds are burnt. He also spoke of darkness such that, in it, one 'wails and gnashes one's teeth'. Moreover, 'the place where the fire burns' is mentioned no less than eight times in the Gospel. He did not tell us of this place to frighten us but to bring it to our notice, in order to warn us. Jesus could not lie. He died to save us. He died for the truth. Hell is therefore a terrible reality, which we can avoid, not by denying it but by allowing our lives to be guided by the grace of Jesus.

Our world and our life would be unimaginable without love. Life is only true life through love. The strength of love is extraordinarily great. To take just one example, there was a mother in Belgium who recently ran through great flames into a burning house to save her child. Without love, life would be nothing short of a hell. Now we have come to the definition of the state of hell that is the true one. Hell is lack of love. We can now also define 'Paradise': it is the state of love. It is God, for God is love. He even loved the world so dearly that He sacrificed His only Son in order to give us true life in Him.

It follows that a denial of Paradise is a denial of love. This would be like denying the sun, the source of life for us and the world. Paradise is love, perfect love. Love exists. The state of love exists. It cannot be made to disappear. We are in contact with love when we lead a Christian life, so that God is with us. We can only understand it fully, however, when we die and are resurrected, when our way of seeing everything will be different. We are very imperfect as long as we live in the world. The next world is a new one, beyond anything we know. Jesus nevertheless revealed it to us and died for it, so that we may one day reach it. In His parables of the royal wedding feast, He has given us a foretaste of what awaits us.

These things are what Jesus has told us about Paradise and hell. Are we in a position to say He was wrong and He did not know what He was talking about? Did He want to deceive us? Why would He want to? When St Paul was in the third Heaven, he saw that God has prepared for the souls who love God 'what no eye has seen and no ear has heard ...'. It can only be love unlimited, which we cannot imagine until we experience it. Love of this order, God's love, longs to have other souls besides Himself that are blissfully happy too, provided, of course, the souls are in agreement with what God wants to give them.

The Queen of Peace tirelessly advises us to decide for Paradise:

The apparitions of the Queen of Peace have been taking place since 1981. She, our loving Mother, is worried about our salvation and so she warns us of dangers and encourages us to decide for what will help us and others to be saved and to live as God wishes. Every apparition is meant to help us, for example by reminding us of what her Son, the Son of God, recommends and of the Gospel, the teachings of the Church and the reality of the next world. She would like to have all of us there with her for eternity; we are her children. She teaches us to pray, encourages us to atone for what has offended God, recommends unwavering faith, shares secrets with us and shows us how she, as our Mother, loves us dearly. She guides us on the path to salvation and holiness.

As in other places in the world where she has appeared, Our Lady has shown the visionaries in Medjugorje places beyond the grave: Paradise, hell and purgatory.

Our Lady has said of Paradise that it is a condition into which those of us go who lived as Jesus wishes us to live. All those who found their peace and joy in Jesus, in what He recommends, will find eternal peace and joy, their salvation, in Paradise, in Him. Paradise will be the great reward for everything we patiently endured in life out of love for God and thus for Jesus. It is worth believing in God, living in a way that is based on true, living faith, avoiding all sin and always being in the state of grace.

The condition of hell is that with which those people punish themselves who lived with serious sin in their soul and died with it in their soul, unrepentant. They excluded themselves from love and eternal happiness. It is terrible to know that there are people who want to belong to Satan and do not change their mind, even on their death bed. How misguided can a person become!

Our Lady has expressly said, in some of her messages, why she has come to visit us in these fateful days:

"Dear children! Again today I call you to consecrate your life to me with love, so I am able to guide you with love. I love you, dear children, with a special love and I desire to bring you all to Heaven unto God. I want you to realize that this life lasts briefly compared with the one in Heaven. Therefore, dear children, decide again today for God. Only that way will I be able to show how much you are dear to me and how much I desire all to be saved and to be with me in Heaven." (27.11.1986)

"Dear children! Today I wish to call you to pray daily for souls in purgatory. For every soul prayer and grace is necessary to reach God and the love of God. By doing this, dear children, you obtain new intercessors who will help you in life to realize that all the earthly things are not important for you, that only Heaven is that for which it is necessary to strive. Therefore, dear children, pray without ceasing that you may be able to help yourselves and the others to whom your prayers will bring joy." (6.11.1986)

"Dear children! Today again I am calling you to pray with your whole heart and day by day to change your life. Especially, dear children, I am calling that by your prayers and sacrifices you begin to live in holiness, because I desire that each one of you who has been to this fountain of grace will come to Paradise with the special gift which you shall give me, and that is holiness. Therefore, dear children, pray and daily change your life in order to become fully holy. I shall always be close to you." (13.11.1986)

"Dear children! I am calling every one of you to start living in God's love. Dear children, you are ready to commit sin, and to put yourselves in the hand of Satan without reflecting. I call on each one of you to consciously decide for God and against Satan. I am your Mother and, therefore, I want to lead you all to perfect holiness. I want each one of you to be happy here on earth and to be with me in Heaven. That is, dear children, the purpose of my coming here and it's my desire." (25.5.1987)

"Dear children! Today also I want to call you all to prayer. Let prayer be your life. Dear children, dedicate your time only to Jesus and He will give you everything that you are seeking. He will reveal Himself to you in fullness. Dear children, Satan is strong and is waiting to test each one of you. Pray, and that way he will neither be able to injure you nor block you on the way of holiness. Dear children, through prayer grow all the more toward God from day to day." (25.11.1987)

"Dear children! Today again I am calling you to prayer and complete surrender to God. You know that I love you and am coming here out of love so I can show you the path to peace and salvation for your souls. I want you to obey me and not permit Satan to seduce you. Dear children, Satan is very strong and, therefore, I ask you to dedicate your prayers to me so that those who are under his influence can be saved. Give witness by your life. Sacrifice your lives for the salvation of the world. I am with you, and I am grateful to you, but in heaven you shall receive the Father's reward which He has promised to you. Therefore, dear children, do not be afraid. If you pray, Satan cannot injure you even a little bit because you are God's children and He is watching over you. Pray and let the rosary always be in your hand as a sign to Satan that you belong to me." (25.2.1988)

"Dear Children! Today I invite all of you who have heard my message of peace to realize it with seriousness and with love in your life. There are many who think that they are doing a lot by talking about the messages, but do not live them. Dear children, I invite you to life and to change all the negative in you, so that it all turns into the positive and life. Dear children, I am with you and I desire to help each of you to live and by living, to witness the good news. I am here, dear children, to help you and to lead you to heaven, and in heaven is the joy through which you can already live heaven now." (25.5.1991)

Examples of the countless overwhelming occurrences that demonstrate the existence of Paradise and hell:

A message of joy from beyond the grave:

There were two sisters (siblings) who had lived for a long time in a convent. The younger one was on her death bed when her sister asked this of her: to be told where she had gone after she died! She replied that, though it is difficult to communicate from eternity, she would do so if the dear Lord were to allow it.

Soon after that, she died; it was 15 October. The older sister prayed each day for her younger sister. Hoping for a sign from her still, on All Souls' Day she heard some steps near her while she was praying. Looking towards the door, she saw nobody but she heard her sister say, "Sister, I am in Heaven! I am not very near Jesus because I did my work only out of duty and habit and I did not show others enough love. Those who love Jesus most in their earthly life will be nearest to Him in the next life. How ever we lead our life, we shall be rewarded accordingly." This was news from the other world, both comforting and a recommendation to us all.

It is very important how conscientiously we do our work, for God, for others and for ourselves. We are advised to do our duties in honour of God and to bear everything patiently out of love, as Jesus did. We will be amply rewarded for the love we gave to God and to other people.

A Polish noble came to believe in the immortality of the soul:

There was a nobleman who used to be aggressive towards those who were believers in the immortality of the soul. One day he was walking in the woods, to get fresh air but also inspiration for arguments against this Christian doctrine.

There he saw a woman gathering firewood and they started speaking to one another. The woman said she was sad that she did not have enough money to buy a Holy Mass for her recently deceased husband. The nobleman, out of sympathy, then gave her the money for the Mass.

A few days later, the nobleman was in his study writing his book with arguments against the doctrine of the immortality of the soul, when a man appeared before him and said, "I have come to thank you for giving my wife the money for the Holy Mass." He then disappeared.

The nobleman became very uneasy and asked his servants how they could possibly have let a stranger in to see him. They replied that they had let nobody in. The noble then sent for the woman he had met that day and had helped with his money. He asked her for a description of her dead husband and, through it, the noble recognized the man he had seen.

The noble thereupon burned all the notes he had made against the belief in the immortality of the soul. He became a champion of the faith and of the doctrine of eternal life.

A mother returned from Paradise to get help for her son:

In the parish of 'Holy Mother Mary' in Zagreb, Chaplain Joseph Lang (later Bishop Lang) was sitting in the parsonage with another priest when into the courtyard came a woman all in black. She asked Chaplain Lang if he would kindly come and visit a sick man. He asked her whether it was urgent and was told it was not so very urgent. He agreed to go and obtained the address, saying he would be there in an hour.

When he arrived at the address, the family were having lunch. He asked for the sick man but nobody knew who it could be, assuring him they were all quite well. They thought he must have mistaken the address. He was sure he had not and, noticing a photo on the wall, told them the woman in the photo had asked him to visit a sick man at that address.

The father of the family went pale. It was his mother in the photo and she had passed into eternity a few years previously. He then said he wanted to make a confession, which he did for the first time after many years. By three o'clock that afternoon, the man was dead.

Help was fetched in time through grace:

A Catholic priest in London was about to retire for the night when the doorbell rang. It was 3 November, 1888. On opening the door, he saw a woman in brown who said, "There is a young man about to die; please go to him quickly!"

The girl who opened the door to the priest assured him there was nobody dying there and that they were all well. She thought it must have been a mistake. The priest assured her he had been given that address; then he apologized and began to pray.

At that moment, a voice was heard from a room, asking the priest to come in and talk, since he was there anyhow. The priest found it was a young man who had called him and he sat down with him. It was the brother of the girl

200   This is the Time of Grace

who had opened the door. The priest spoke to him about general things and also about the faith. The young man admitted he was not a believer and only prayed one Hail Mary every evening, as he had learnt from his mother. He had done so to that day but that was all.

The discussion went on into the night but, in the course of it, the young man began to change his attitude to the faith, through grace and our dear Heavenly Mother. Finally he made a confession of his whole life and also promised to go to Holy Communion the next day. When the next day dawned, however, he could no longer go to Communion, having died peacefully that same night.

Father Petar and Father Jozo Zovko

This is the Time of Grace

PART FOUR

A prayer said by a person as best he can
has great power.
It makes a bitter heart sweet,
a sad one glad, a poor one rich,
a foolish one wise, a despairing one brave,
a weak one strong, a blind one see,
a cold one burn!

It draws the great God
into a small heart;
it bears a hungry soul
aloft to God, the living source
and brings together two who
love one another!

(Gertrud von Helfta)

Prayer for Healing

In order to be able to pray for healing, it is important to have complete faith in Jesus Christ. Let us open all our wounds to Him and give them to Him, praying: **Jesus, if it is Your will, You can heal me in body and soul.... Jesus, have mercy on me, have mercy on all those who are now imploring You.... Look upon my wounds. Heal them and send Your Spirit upon me!**

Lord Jesus Christ, I believe that You are present at this moment. I place all my hope in You and I love You above all else. I ask You to bless me and to bless this whole place. Grant me the gift of prayer. May Your Sacred Blood cleanse me of all sin, free me of fear and remove from me everything that obstructs the path leading to You!

Come, Holy Spirit and fill me with Your strength. Come and instruct me! Come and enlighten me! May Your Spirit exert Its powerful influence on me and on the Church. May It make all things new.

Jesus, I now lay my whole past before You. I place it all in Your hands, starting from the moment I was born.

You know all the bad qualities I inherited from my parents, grandparents and great grandparents. I thank You for my mother and my father. I forgive them for everything and ask You to forgive them too, if their love for me was insufficient. I pray that You will save them and guide them to Paradise, so that we may one day rejoice together in Your presence!

Jesus, I place my complete trust and all my hope in You, my God and Saviour!

This is the Time of Grace

I place my whole future in Your hands. I do not know what awaits me in my life. You, however, know all things and You are guiding me.

I now place my present time of life in Your hands. May it belong only to You. I surrender to You my soul, my spirit and my body, my mind and my will, my blood and my heart, my feelings and my spiritual capabilities!

Take into Your hands my work and my leisure time, my failures, my plans and wishes, my habits and all my dependencies…!

Jesus, I give You all my sins, from childhood up to the present day! Jesus, I am sorry I have sinned and offended God so often! You know I am weak and sinful. I sincerely repent of all my sins!

Here, in Your presence, I renounce every sin, every negative thought, especially bad words and deeds…!

I renounce all lack of faith, all complaining, all cursing, all immorality and enmity! I renounce all dealings with the occult, soothsaying, magic and all fear!

Jesus, thank You for receiving and hearing my prayer!

Thank You for loving me and desiring to help me! Thank You for accepting me just as I am! Thank You for knowing that I wish to be different and live as You would have me live!

Jesus, in the power of Your grace, I accept this life of mine and I thank the Lord for every gift! I ask for forgiveness for not always having accepted my life and what my life has brought me according to Your will!

I was angry and irritable, envious and jealous. I wish never to be like this again! Jesus, help me...! I accept myself now as I truly am. I forgive myself for everything I have not been able to forgive myself for up to now. You know I have experienced circumstances that were difficult and painful.

You have forgiven me for everything and therefore I forgive myself. From now on I wish to live in the light of faith and in Your grace!

For this reason I forgive all those who have ever hurt me, whether consciously or unconsciously! Forgive them too, 0 Jesus!

Come to the aid of my faith and strengthen it...! Heal what is half-hearted in my faith! Renew and enhance our faith in You, our Saviour! Grant that my hope and my trust in You be unlimited!

Let me be filled with hope! Give me the grace to hope that You can change all misery, all affliction and all distress for the better.

Let the flame of Your divine love ignite me with love for You, Your beloved Father, the Holy Spirit and all of my brothers and sisters...!

With unwavering, living faith and filled with trust, I turn to You, O my dearest and most merciful Jesus and I beseech You...!

Give me the grace to be guided by love in my work, in all that I undertake and in my whole life!

With unwavering, living faith and filled with trust, I beg You, Jesus, to cleanse me of my flaws and sins through Your most Sacred Blood! Absolve me of my trespasses and deliver me from all evil! Free me of all my failings and of all things that keep me from You!

I ask You, Jesus, to release me from all sinful dependencies!

Release me and all of us from every curse and every sin! Release me from all sexual dependencies, satanic influences and bonds!

Release me from all occult works (card reading, palm reading, soothsaying) and from all magic!

Release me from idolatry, from anger, from the feeling that my life is meaningless! Free me of the tendency to criticize others and to speak ill of them! Release me from nicotine and alcohol consumption and from drug addiction! Release me and cure me of all sinful habits!

Jesus, You are my great brother! You are my Lord and my God! You are my best doctor! You are the one who can never betray me! Thank You for being so good and kind to us…!

Thanks be to You, 0 Jesus, for having taken my sins, illnesses and sufferings upon yourself! In so doing, You have reconciled me with God. I am miraculously saved; through Your wounds I am healed…!

You are healing me today too, through Your grace, which You earned for me on the cross….

Filled with trust and filled with faith, I beg You: lay Your divine hand on me and heal my broken heart!

Lay Your holy hand on each painful wound…. Speak but one word and every wound will be healed. One word will suffice. You are our God, who can do all things!!!

Lord Jesus Christ, heal my sick body!!!

Through Your most Sacred Blood, which You shed for us and through the power of Your holy wounds, I beg You to heal my soul and my spirit…!

For the sake of Your crown of thorns and the pain that You suffered for me, heal all illnesses of the brain, spine and nerves…!

Lay Your hand upon me and, with Your divine light and Your healing power, heal all tumours and every incurable disease. Restore my cells to the healthy condition that You gave them in the beginning…!

Place Your fingers in my ears and open them, so that I may hear You, take Your Word seriously and live according to it…!

Jesus, speak but one word and my paralysed limbs will carry me with renewed strength…!

For the sake of the wounds that You suffered in Your hands and feet, remove from me all illnesses of the joints, muscles, sinews, bones and ligaments…!

Reach out and touch the afflicted areas of my skin. Cleanse me and make me well…!

May the water flowing from Your side renew me and be my blessing! Strengthen my heart, purify my blood and heal the unhealthy vessels…!

Heal my ailing kidneys, my bladder, my reproductive organs…! Heal the glands and hormones…!

This is the Time of Grace

Heal all illnesses of the stomach and bowel, the liver and the gall bladder...! Remove all illnesses of the breathing passages and lungs...!

Jesus, strengthen everything in me that is weak! Make everything underdeveloped grow normally...!

Strengthen my immune system and remove all infection from me...!

Fill me with all the gifts of the Holy Spirit, so that in You, Lord, I have life, life to the full! Grant peace to all peoples and to each individual person...!

Give me, through Your grace, the ability to grow in faith, hope and love...!

Lord, I now present to You, with faith, all the sick people who have asked me to pray for them....

You love them all. You know them all.... You know of their illnesses and their great sufferings....

I beg of You: bless them and help them! Relieve their sufferings and restore them to health...!

I beg You to have mercy on them! Have mercy on all those who are suffering in their body or soul! Be gracious and merciful to them all! Heal them all, dear Lord and Saviour!

Jesus, I implore You through the mediation of our Mother, the Queen of Peace! You gave her to us for her to be our Mother and You have also sent her to us.

Queen of Peace, our Mother, pray for me and for all other people and commend us to your Son!

Jesus, for the sake of Your heavenly Father's name, I ask You to enlighten all of humanity; free us, heal us, save us...!

Heal and save all the sick people who hear this prayer and pray it...! Glorify Your Father in us all! May Your Kingdom come into our hearts... May Your will be done regarding us.... Remove all temptations from us.

Give me and everybody our daily bread and everything we need for our eternal salvation! You can do everything! Nothing is impossible for You! This is in accordance with Your will! You are our God! Your love for us is unlimited! You are still here with us!

Without You I can do nothing! With You I can do all things!

I believe in You completely! I trust in You! I love You above all else!

I ask You to stay with me always, protect me, accompany me, keep me and guide me to eternal life!

Through the mediation of our heavenly Mother Mary and all saints, bless and heal me, O almighty God, the Father, the Son and the Holy Spirit. Amen!

Adoration of the Most Holy Sacrament

P: Blessed be Jesus eternally
C: In the Most Holy Sacrament!

Blessed be the Father who sent You, for You to sacrifice Yourself for us in this way!
Blessed be the Holy Spirit, exclaiming within us: blessed be God in all eternity!

Blessed be that moment, Lord Jesus, in which You, on Maundy Thursday, established the Holy Eucharist.
We adore You, O Jesus, here and in all churches the world over, in all chapels and before all tabernacles. We thank You unceasingly for Your remaining with us in this way.

We adore You, we praise You, we thank You for Your endless love. We adore You and thank You for thinking of us always and waiting for us. Thank You for always having time for us.
We believe You are here with us now. Humbly we beg You: help us in our lack of faith! Strengthen us, give us complete faith! Give us faith that enables us always to recognize You, You who are here, concealed in this sanctified bread.

We fully believe You are true God and true Man. We believe You are powerful, that You can do all things. Therefore we are here before You. We wish to show You our love and our faithfulness.
We adore You with our whole being, with body and soul, with all our heart, with all our strength. We surrender to You entirely. We entrust our innermost secrets to You. We dedicate to You each day and each moment of our life.

Jesus, we now dedicate and surrender everything to You: our families, our possessions, our health, our work, our capabilities, our time, our successes and failures. We entrust to You our will: all the plans and wishes we have for ourselves and others.

We surrender our weaknesses to You, Jesus, our fears, uncertainties and everything that burdens us. We surrender our whole life to You, our past, our present and our future. In illness and in health, in life and in death we are Yours!

We adore You and thank You for being allowed to surrender everything to You. You accept us as we are. You know we would like to be better than we are. We would like to try to fulfil the heavenly Father's will. Teach us always to live honestly! Teach us to love You with sincerity and to stay faithful to You always! Never allow us to forget You! Please, Jesus, help us! Please give us strength; give us endurance and goodness, in Your name!

We are prepared; we accept everything. May only Your will be done, regarding us and all other people. We wish for nothing else, O Lord!

Jesus, You know of all our burdens, our torments, our sufferings and pains. You suffer with all those who are suffering and You rejoice with all those who are joyful. You share our sadness and weariness. You take our needs seriously and You understand our passions. You are delighted when we forgive one another and are reconciled. You are aware of all the unfulfilled yet justified requests that we have. We adore You, 0 Jesus; we ask You to free us of our tiredness and lack of concentration. Take from us all our worries, fears and sufferings; grant us relief from our afflictions. Keep us from all temptations and all evil!

This is the Time of Grace

We adore You, O Jesus Christ, and thank You for hearing our prayers. We thank You for being our path through life! You are the only truth in our life! You are true life and our resurrection!

We adore You, Jesus, and we thank You for this Sacrament of Holy Love! At this moment in the Adoration, let us experience the great mystery of Your immeasurable love. You came to be with us out of love for us. You lived but a short time on earth. You came in order to turn this vale of tears into Heaven for us, with the whole of humanity one family in God and every human being a child of God. You brought us the fire of Holy Love and it is Your wish that this fire enflame the hearts of all of us.

We adore You, Lord Jesus Christ, and we thank You for being allowed to communicate with You and worship You. To be with You is pure joy. You are love and goodness itself. You accept everyone and reject not a single soul. For You, none is such a great sinner that You would not love him, welcome him, heal him and save him. You suffer too when someone suffers. You are sympathetic towards anyone who is sad or in despair.

Jesus, You said to us, 'What shall it profit a man, to gain the whole world and forfeit his soul?' (Mark 8, 36) Truly, O Jesus, everything else perishes and saving the soul is the only worthwhile thing. The soul is of more value than all the treasures in the world put together. In this vale of tears, the saving of the soul is our most important task. Jesus, thank You for these words; we shall never forget them.

Jesus, our Saviour, we adore You and we beg You to free us of all our dependencies. Renew us and strengthen us! Relieve all sufferings and heal all wounds! We wish now to be freed and to find our peace, our joy and our salvation only in You! Create in us a new heart and grant us all the gift of Your Spirit! Thank You for hearing our prayer!

We adore You, 0 Jesus, and beg You to forgive us for giving You so little thanks for all Your gifts and for all You do for us. You are our best and dearest friend. We hear Your voice anew, saying, 'Come to me, all who labour and are heavy laden, and I will give you rest.' (Matt. 11, 28) Thank You, Jesus, for these words! We now know who to turn to in our sufferings. Sometimes we are more than tired, fearful and depressed, Lord Jesus; sometimes we see no way out of our situation; yet You are there and it is beyond question that You invite us to approach You. We are here before You, Lord and Saviour!

You are the true Bread that came from Heaven; whoever eats this Bread of Life will live in eternity. This Bread is Your Most Holy Body, which is our Life and the Life of the world. We wish now to receive You spiritually, knowing that, if we receive You in faith, we shall have eternal Life. Thus we are here and long for You with all our being! Jesus, You are the Bread of Life, the health of body and soul! Be our peace, our consolation, our victory and our strength! Thank You, Lord Jesus, for being our King and being the source of all holiness, of perfect security and our life's fulfilment!

Blessed be Jesus Christ in this Most Holy Sacrament! We praise You, knowing that Your love for us has no bounds; thus You sacrificed Your life in order to give us Life; we know Your Precious Blood has cleansed us and given us salvation; we know You came to save what was lost and to call the sinners, to give them Life in You, O Lord. Blessed be Lord Jesus! You know us, Lord, yet You still have such faith in us and invite us to strive for holiness and perfection.

This is the Time of Grace

Blessed be Jesus Christ! Lord, You wish us to have an honest and humble heart, so that You can fill it with love and mercy; Lord, may You pour out Your love and Your gifts upon it once more, so we may begin anew.
Blessed be Lord Jesus! Your love and Your forgiveness, Lord, are greater than our weakness and fragility. You are the giver of life and You constantly renew Your mercy.

Blessed be Jesus Christ! You constantly touch our heart and invite us to return to You, so that we may receive Your forgiveness and Your gifts of love.
Blessed be Lord Jesus! You invite us to start afresh and receive life, forgiveness, love and joy from You. Lord, You gave us this impulse; we, in turn, ask You to be near us. Enlightened and guided by Your Holy Spirit, may we always seek You and remain faithful and devoted to You.

You, Lord, gave us this impulse; we seek our salvation in You. We implore You to let it be fulfilled. Amen.

Prayer of total devotion to Jesus:

O Lord Jesus Christ, You were the first to sacrifice Yourself for us completely. You loved us to the bitter end, to death on the cross. You have remained with us and You will be with us to the last of all days in the Most Holy Sacrament of Your Love.
Jesus, I now dedicate myself entirely to You. I thank You for all the gifts of Your Love that I have received.

I wish today to renew my trust in You and to thank You for my Baptism. I renew the promise of my Baptism and I wish to live as You require of me. Filled with joy and gratitude, I recognize God as my Heavenly Father.

Lord, grant me from today all the gifts of the Holy Spirit, so that I may fulfil Your wishes for me. Grant me Your grace, so that, like our Blessed Mother Mary, I may be Your true servant. Grant that we all may finally meet in Your Heavenly Kingdom, where we shall praise You for all eternity! Amen.

Stations of the Cross of our Lord Jesus Christ

Introductory Prayer

We are gathered here with faith before You, Jesus, to walk the stations of the cross with You. You took Your cross upon Yourself joyfully and died on it. In so doing, You appeased God and atoned for our sins. If You had not done so, we would not be here. We would have no hope of going to Paradise. We would be condemned to eternal death.

You Yourself said: 'Whoever wishes to be My follower, let him deny himself, daily take his cross upon himself and follow Me.' (Luke 9,23) Thus You have called me to follow You and be converted to You.

You know me, dear Saviour. You know my capabilities and my weaknesses. Without You I can do nothing! Today I would like to gather strength from the stations of Your cross for my own life's path. I know I must climb my own Mount of Calvary each day. My Saviour, how hard it is!

Now, at this moment, I beg You to help me! I ask this of You for all the others, too, who are finding life difficult. Bless us all, convert us, make us holy, free us and change us! Be near us, give us a renewed heart and Your Holy Spirit!

May this contemplation of Your sufferings help us to reach safely the harbour of eternal salvation! Queen of Peace, we beg you to accompany us as we walk the stations of the cross!

1st Station: Jesus is condemned to death.

P: We adore You O Christ and praise You,
C: Because by Your holy cross You have redeemed the world.

Jesus, You were condemned to death. It is terrible to be condemned, especially if one is innocent. Is it then possible, Lord, to remain so loving and at peace in one's soul as You did? One can. You demonstrated this to me. I thank You!

Lord, keep me from all judging and condemning! I ask You especially not to permit me to condemn anyone to death in my heart, to eliminate him from my life and disappoint him.

Jesus, grant me the grace of preferring to be condemned myself rather than judge others; to suffer misery rather than inflict it on another person!

From all evil,	Lord, free us!
From all sin,	Lord, free us!
From anger and hate,	Lord, free us!
From all defamation,	Lord, free us!
From all slander,	Lord, free us!
From all condemnation,	Lord, free us!
From eternal damnation,	Lord, free us!

Mother of our Lord, our Mother, pray for us, so that we may always say, as you did: 'Lord, let it be unto me as You say.'

P: Crucified Lord Jesus Christ,
C: Have mercy on us and on the whole world!

2nd Station: Jesus takes up the heavy cross.

P: We adore You O Christ and praise You,
C: Because by Your holy cross You have redeemed the world.

You were the first to accept the cross absolutely voluntarily and joyfully. Since then, the cross has become a source of salvation for us. It is the sign and the safeguard of our salvation. All the sins of the world together with our own sins are what carved and moulded the cross. Jesus accepted it, in order to die on it for us. He made it into an altar of love, which liberates, revives, heals and saves. All the torment and sin of the earth plus all of Heaven's love were poured into the cross.

Divine Saviour, with the cross on Your shoulder, You opened up a new path. True, it is the path of the cross, yet it is also love's path of salvation. Should I, Jesus, simply refuse my cross and all the crosses near me?

Jesus, help me to grasp all the value of the cross and the treasure hidden in it! Grant me the grace of accepting joyfully any cross sent to me by Your providence.

Forgive me, Jesus, for burdening Your shoulder with the cross; this was whenever I was unfair and impatient towards others or I wanted to take revenge and whenever I left it to others to do what was really my duty.

P: Crucified Lord Jesus Christ,
C: Have mercy on us and on the whole world!

3rd Station: Jesus falls for the first time.

P: We adore You O Christ and praise You,
C: Because by Your holy cross You have redeemed the world.

Jesus stumbles and falls under the cross. We do not know if You fell because of the weight of the cross or through physical exhaustion. You agreed to be weak; You wanted to be one with us in that way. It was hard for You to see how Your followers and friends left You and Your own people accused You and demanded You receive the maximum penalty. It was very bitter for You to have to endure the people's ingratitude.

Jesus, You lay but a short time on the ground. You stood up again and continued to carry Your cross, walking on towards Your destination. Why did You let that happen right at the beginning of Your path to Calvary?

Through this fall I would like to learn something very important. If I fall through a misfortune on my life's path, I beg You to grant me the grace of managing, with You, to continue walking! Nothing should ever discourage me from following You along the path.

Jesus, give all those the strength to go on who are feeling their weakness and uncertainty! We ask You to give this strength to all those who have already fallen but do not know how to stand up again! Convert all those who have lost their faith, so that they trust in Your grace once again.

P: Crucified Lord Jesus Christ,
C: Have mercy on us and on the whole world!

This is the Time of Grace

4th Station: Jesus meets His Mother.

P: We adore You O Christ and praise You,
C: Because by Your holy cross You have redeemed the world.

Jesus, as You walk with Your cross, You are accompanied by Your Mother. Mary is always present where the will of God is done. Just as You said: 'Not My will but Thy will be done', so Your Mother, too, had pronounced her 'Fiat! I am the handmaid of the Lord; let it be unto me as You say.' Because Your Mother was with You as You carried Your cross, she carried it too. As the Mother of the Church, she is there with every single one of us as we carry our cross.

Mary, you wanted to help your Son more, whom you loved so much, but you could not. All you could do was suffer with Him. I thank you, Mother of our Lord, for having come to be with us in these difficult times, which are being shattered by crises. You call on us tirelessly to be converted and do penance, to fast and pray, to have strong faith in God and to be reconciled with God and our fellow beings, so that we have peace, joy, happiness and eternal salvation.

Dear Mother, we beg you to stay with us as we bear our cross. Be near us, especially when trials and temptations come or when God desires a sacrifice of us.

Let us pray for all mothers who are sad and in despair on account of their children! May your Son console them and save everyone!

P: Crucified Lord Jesus Christ,
C: Have mercy on us and on the whole world!

This is the Time of Grace

5th Station: Simon helps Jesus to carry the cross.

P: We adore You O Christ and praise You,
C: Because by Your holy cross You have redeemed the world.

Lord Jesus, how difficult it was for You! You were at the end of Your strength. You could not carry Your cross any farther. There were plenty people accompanying You but only Simon really helped You in this way. He was returning from his field, perhaps on his way home. Perhaps he was very tired, yet he still helped You.

Forgive me, Jesus, for constantly forgetting that the cross frees us from evil and that it unites, reconciles and saves us. Jesus, please forgive me for avoiding the cross, thereby avoiding being loving! Jesus, please forgive me for constantly making the excuse that I am too tired or have no time to do something or I want to put it off until later.

Lord Jesus, please grant me the humility and the will always to be prepared to accept a 'Simon' on my life's path, so that I may go and stay with You, accompanied by many whom I needed and many who needed me! Lord Jesus, please grant me the grace always to be prepared to do what my conscience tells me and to help anyone in any situation gladly!

Mary, Mother of our Lord, please teach me not to complain but to be joyful because I am carrying the cross with Jesus and am aware that He sees me and blesses me!

P: Crucified Lord Jesus Christ,
C: Have mercy on us and on the whole world!

This is the Time of Grace

6th Station: Veronica hands Jesus the linen face cloth.

P: We adore You O Christ and praise You,
C: Because by Your holy cross You have redeemed the world.

A woman called Veronica could not resist her heartfelt wish to go nearer Jesus as He suffered and offer Him her sympathy. She wanted to show her love and for this she was rewarded. Out of gratitude, our Saviour left an image of His holy countenance on the cloth she handed to Him for Him to wipe His face.

Veronica contemplated the bloodstained, tortured face of Jesus in His sufferings and, in doing so repeatedly, she helped many others. You, Lord, wish to teach me something through this. Jesus, grant me the grace to be able to recognize You in all those I live and work with. This is not always easy. Some faces are displeasing to me. There are some faces I do not wish to look at and I turn my head away. Some faces seem to me to be tedious and a problem. However You, Jesus, are concealed in every person and You want us to recognize Yourself in every face. Give us a heart like Veronica's!

I pray to You, Jesus, for all women, mothers, girls and sisters. Without them, life and our world could not be sustained. Bless them and make them holy! Keep them safe, so that they may always be pure and holy like Veronica. Remove from them all temptations, so that they may not be seducers and temptresses.

Do not let us hide Your face away in our soul from those who do not yet know You. Help us to be Your disciples, so that everyone may recognize You in us!
P: Crucified Lord Jesus Christ,
C: Have mercy on us and on the whole world!

7th Station: Jesus falls for the second time.

P: We adore You O Christ and praise You,
C: Because by Your holy cross You have redeemed the world.

P: Lord Jesus, the second fall was harder and more painful than the first. Your tiredness and weakness were increasing, as was the fear that was gripping Your heart. Our lack of faith, our ingratitude and our great sins like cursing, blaspheming, drunkenness, divorce and unchastity caused You such great sufferings.

Jesus, how many of us are even now in a state of serious sin?! Have mercy, Jesus, on all great sinners, convert them and save them. A great many young people have lost their faith; their ideals are crushed, their souls poisoned with drugs, alcohol and sins. Only You can help the young people! Help everyone!

Jesus, I thank You for being the lamb of God that takes away the sin of the world, for standing up again under the weight of Your cross and for continuing to carry it.

Give me the strength to stand up again with You after a repeated fall and to continue walking with You faithfully and patiently. Let me not find that sin destroys me, once I have resolved not to sin again. Encourage me to walk on and on with You.

P: Crucified Lord Jesus Christ,
C: Have mercy on us and on the whole world!

This is the Time of Grace

8th Station: Jesus consoles the weeping women.

P: We adore You O Christ and praise You,
C: Because by Your holy cross You have redeemed the world.

Lord Jesus, the weeping women saw You passing by, covered in blood and totally exhausted. They were sorry for You and wanted to help You but they could not. You were very grateful to them for everything, however at this moment You pointed out to them that sin was the cause of Your dreadful torment.

You said: 'Weep for yourselves and your children!' Did the women grasp the meaning of this? We do not know. Did they know what was awaiting them and their sons?

It is easy to find the sins of others repellent, yet it is hard to weep over our own sins! Forgive me, Jesus, for not yet having wept over my sins! Forgive me for not managing to have others recognize Your presence in me! Forgive me for not enabling others to find Your love in me!

Come, Lord Jesus, into my heart and my house; my door is open to You! Come and grant me the gift of tears, through which to repent of my sins! Cleanse my soul, that I may find in You peace, joy, happiness and eternal salvation!

P: Crucified Lord Jesus Christ,
C: Have mercy on us and on the whole world!

9th Station: Jesus falls for the third time.

P: We adore You O Christ and praise You,
C: Because by Your holy cross You have redeemed the world.

Lord Jesus, Your third fall was the hardest and most painful one. Jesus, You carried the cross and fell beneath it, to save me, my nation and everybody. I thank You! Jesus, I feel the truth of what Saint Paul said: 'Whoever thinks he is standing upright must be careful not to fall!'

Jesus, with this fall You perhaps thought most of those people for whom Your suffering is in vain. You wish Your suffering and death to be the source of life and grace. There are people who despise or reject life. They destroy or damage the lives of others or even their own life.

Jesus, convert me! Convert everyone! To be converted means to decide for the path of faith and prayer. This means standing up again repeatedly in our life and continuing with Jesus. Please complete the work of our salvation that You began, in me and my brothers and sisters.

Protect our families, so that they may be communities of life, joy, peace and happiness! Help everyone who is now in danger of falling!

P: Crucified Lord Jesus Christ,
C: Have mercy on us and on the whole world!

This is the Time of Grace

10th Station: Jesus is divested of His clothing.

P: We adore You O Christ and praise You,
C: Because by Your holy cross You have redeemed the world.

Lord Jesus, why did You allow Your adversaries to divest You of Your clothing? Why did You allow them to offend You so grievously? It seems as if You want to say to us, "Dear friends, why do you dishonour the name 'Christian' through immodest clothing, behaviour and talk and through indecent reading material, pictures and films? In this you are like those who took off My clothes and you only increase My sufferings! Please do not act like this towards Me any more!"

Thank You, Jesus; through being humiliated in this way, You atoned for our sins of unchastity, for all our offences and for everything that brings misfortune upon us.

Jesus, grant me the grace of realizing that my body is a temple of the Holy Spirit and therefore a great mystery. You invested my body with feelings and modesty.

Keep me, Lord, from anything that could 'infect' my body and impair my chastity! Grant me the grace of preserving the mystery of the human body, mine and that of others! It is my wish that my body glorify You!

P: Crucified Lord Jesus Christ,
C: Have mercy on us and on the whole world!

11th Station: Jesus is nailed to the cross.

P: We adore You O Christ and praise You,
C: Because by Your holy cross You have redeemed the world.

Lord Jesus, Your hands and feet were pierced by the sins of mankind. How dreadful this is! Let us genuinely repent of our sins and pray for forgiveness. Let us decide not to sin any more in future!

Lord, You gave us our hands, for us to reach out in honour of Your name; to fold them humbly when we come to You in need. You gave us our hands so that we may do good works today and every day of our life. You gave us our feet so that we can go to the aid of our brother, that is, our neighbour.

You were nearest to me, Lord, when You were hanging on the cross by Your hands and feet, indeed, precisely when You could no longer move. Blessed be Your hands and feet, by which You hung on the cross! They bring blessings to us all. Place me in Your wounds, Lord Jesus!

Soul of Christ, make me holy!
Body of Christ, grant me salvation!
Blood of Christ, satiate me!
Water from Christ's side, cleanse me!
Sufferings of Christ, strengthen me!
O merciful Jesus, hear me! Conceal me in Your wounds!
Never let me leave You! Protect me from the evil one!
At the hour of my death, call me! Bid me to come to You,
To praise You with Your saints, In Your Kingdom eternally!

P: Crucified Lord Jesus Christ,
C: Have mercy on us and on the whole world!

This is the Time of Grace

12th: Station: Jesus dies on the cross.

P: We adore You O Christ and praise You,
C: Because by Your holy cross You have redeemed the world.

Lord Jesus, after suffering bitterly for three hours You died. You died on the cross for everybody. This is the station of Your total sacrifice. You were raised upon the cross, to draw everyone to You.

This is also the station of my life. You invite me to dedicate myself to You. Let me, too, be drawn to You, Jesus! I thank You for sparing Yourself nothing, rather, sacrificing Yourself completely for me. Such is Your wonderful love, Lord, for me!

Lord Jesus, You are splendid in Your works, Your love and Your goodness; I praise You, I laud You and I adore You in the mystery of Your cross. Each cross tells me of You. Each cross calls me to renew my dedication to You. Forgive me, Lord, for being so reticent and so lacking in resolve here before Your cross!

Forgive me, Lord, for counting so little on You and Your love in my life! Forgive me for living so irresponsibly. May I accept the saving grace that You earned for me on the cross. I beseech You at this station: merciful Jesus, think of me and help me to reach Your Kingdom!

P: Crucified Lord Jesus Christ,
C: Have mercy on us and on the whole world.

13th Station: Jesus is laid in the lap of His Mother.

P: We adore You O Christ and praise You,
C: Because by Your holy cross You have redeemed the world.

Lord Jesus, Your body is now in Your Mother's lap. You have completed Your task. You have fulfilled everything Your Father asked of You. How I thank You!

Mary, Mother of Jesus and our Mother, you are the Mother of the Church and the Mother of each one of us. We entrust our wounds and the sufferings in our life to you. Thank you, Mother, for being with us and for staying with us on the path of our life. We know we are not alone.

We beseech you to pray for us, so that all of us praying these stations of the cross may one day be with you in His Kingdom.

C: Holy Mother of God,
We take refuge
Beneath your protecting mantle.
Do not reject our prayer
In our difficulties but
Save us always from all danger.
0 you splendid and blessed virgin,
Our Lady, our mediator,
Our intercessor.
Guide us to your Son,
Commend us to your Son,
Present us to your Son!

P: Crucified Lord Jesus Christ,
C: Have mercy on us and on the whole world!

This is the Time of Grace

14th Station: Jesus is laid in the grave.

P: We adore You O Christ and praise You,
C: Because by Your holy cross You have redeemed the world.

Lord Jesus, You lay in the grave but the grave could not keep You there. You were victorious over the grave. In this way, You unlocked the secret of the grave for us. On the third day You rose again in splendour. Thank You for rising from the grave! Through Your resurrection, You were victorious over death, sin, Satan, evil and suffering. Thus You proved that You are true God and true Man; that everything You said is true; and that we too will be resurrected one day.

You transformed the apparent defeat on the cross into a resounding victory. Your cross became the source of consolation and salvation. Only You can change the darkness of the grave into the light of Easter. Your adversaries became wretched people without hope. Your followers, however, became the happy victors with You.

You said that we will be resurrected too. This is our one great consolation in this vale of tears. Lord Jesus, I thank You for Your death and Your resurrection! I love You beyond all else. I believe in You, in Your resurrection and in my resurrection.

Jesus, we ask You only to grant us the grace of basing our daily life on this faith and of turning each moment of our life into a moment of salvation for ourselves and others.

P: Crucified Lord Jesus Christ,
C: Have mercy on us and on the whole world!

Prayer of Thanksgiving

Lord Jesus, we thank You for the grace of being able to contemplate Your suffering and Your death. We unite our sufferings with Yours and our crosses with Your cross. Grant us the grace of being allowed to be with You in death too.

Jesus, each one of us will now say with greatest sincerity to You:

I renounce every sin! I renounce Satan! I reject everything that leads to death! I wish to live only for You. I wish to lead a meaningful life, so that I may one day have eternal life. My Lord, I am Yours and I remain Yours! Take me and all those who request it of You into Your Kingdom! Amen!

Salvation
was meant to come solely
from the lesson of the cross
from the power of the cross
from love of the cross!

(F. Beat Ambord)

I Believe in the Holy Spirit

I believe that He can annihilate my prejudices.
I believe that He can alter my bad habits.
I believe that He can overcome my indifference.
I believe that He can inspire me to be loving.
I believe that He can warn me of evil.
I believe that He can give me courage to do good.
I believe that He can defeat my sadness.
I believe that He can grant me love of God's Word.
I believe that He can remove feelings of inferiority from me.
I believe that He can give me strength in my life.
I believe that He can send me a brother or sister to help me.
I believe that He can pervade my being.

(Karl Rahner)

Lord God, our Creator

You became man, to be near us.
We have nothing to fear.
In all of life's situations You stay close to us,
Though we may not always see and feel Your presence.
Comfort us when we feel lonely and sad.
Guide us when we are uncertain and confused.
Steady us when we doubt and despair.
Have mercy on us when we are weak and we fail.
Strengthen us in suffering and fear.
Keep us glad to be alive
And accomplish in us, Lord,
What we ourselves cannot do.

In God's Hand

Lord, I seek a hand that holds and encourages me, that calms and protects me.

I grope for a hand that accompanies and guides me, heals and saves me.

I need a hand that is strong and carries me, clasps me and does not let me go.

I wish for a hand that wants the best for me, that tenderly embraces me.

I long for a hand that I can entrust myself to entirely, that is true and loves me.

I seek a great hand in which I can place my small hands and also my heart, a hand

I am safe in - completely.

Lord, Your hand invites me: come!

Your hand lets me feel: do not be afraid!

Your hand gives the assurance: I love you. In Your hand I am safe and saved for ever.

And should I nonetheless fall into an abyss, I know: in the depths of this abyss Your hand awaits me, Your kindly, rescuing hand.

And from Your loving hand no-one can wrench me.

Lord, in Your hand I place all I have.

Your hand will never let me go.

Thank You, You kind, gentle hand, thank You.

Jesus, You grasp hold of the sick with Your hand and right them.

You reach out Your hand to Peter who is sinking and save him.

You tenderly lay Your hand upon the children and bless them.

You show Your wounded hands to the sad disciples and say: 'Behold and understand!'

Jesus, clasp me too with Your hand.

For in Your hand all is well! (Theo Schmiedkonz SJ)

Prayer for our Children

Lord Jesus Christ,
Through the hands of Your holy Mother, we consecrate our children and our young people to You!
Through the mediation of Mary, help them find their way back to You.
Deliver them from atheism and selfishness!
Keep them from harm to body and soul!
Protect them from the tempters of our time!
Heal the wounds they received through this society!
Call some of them to be saints!
Send us the Holy Spirit, so that we do not lose courage when we know not what to do.
Forgive us for the times we failed to love them and be an example to them!
Strengthen us where we are weak!
Console us where all consolation has gone!
Lord Jesus Christ,
Through the hands of Your holy Mother, we consecrate our children and our young people to You!

Daily Prayer to the Holy Family

Jesus, paragon of exalted virtues, exemplary and loving in Your family life on earth, You made Your chosen family a holy one.

Look graciously upon our family kneeling before you and imploring You for grace.

Remember that this family belongs to You, having given and consecrated themselves entirely to serving You.

Graciously protect them, save them from all danger, help them in all their problems and give them the strength always to follow the example of Your holy family.

Grant that they remain faithful to serving You and loving You their whole lives and afterwards praise You eternally in Heaven.

0 Mary, loving Mother, we ask you for your protection, firmly believing that your godly Son will hear your petitions.

Saint Joseph, wonderful patriarch, help us, lend us your powerful support too and present, through Mary's hands, our petitions to Christ.

I Need You Lord

Lord, I need You every day!
Give me living faith,
That I may be near You!

Give me living hope,
That I may be guided
By the promises You gave us!

Give me living love,
That I may pass Your love on
To other people!

Lord, I need You every day:
In the morning, during the day
And in the evening!

At night time too I need You!
May Your love keep me safe,
Now and every day and for eternity!
Amen!

This is the Time of Grace

Prayers of Thanksgiving with Complete Dedication

Lord, I thank You for everything

Lord, I thank You for the gift of life, for every grace I have received!
Lord, I place myself entirely in Your hands.
Do as You would with me.
Help me to live according to Your will and to be prepared to do what You expect of me.
I wish to be what You want me for and all that You want to turn me into.
I surrender myself to You, for You to lead me where You would.
I wish to follow You in the darkness and ask only for strength for each new day.

Lord, may we do Your Will

Take, Lord, our body, that we may patiently endure its weaknesses.
Take, Lord, our spirit, that we may, in Your light, believe in You more and more.
Take, Lord, our heart, that we may love You above all else.
Take, Lord, our will, that we may fulfil Your will.
Take, Lord, our freedom, that we may not decide against You.
Take, Lord, our strength, that we may serve You with our life.
Take, Lord, our cross and sufferings, that they may be fruitful in our salvation.
Take, Lord, all that we are and have. Amen!

Prayer for Peace

Mother of mercy, plead for us to God for the Christian reconciliation of peoples!

Let especially those graces be effective that can instantly change the hearts of people, the graces that prepare and assure the peace we long for!

Queen of Peace, pray for us and give the world peace in Christ's truth, justice and love!

Give the world above all peace in the soul, so that the Kingdom of God be extended in quiet orderliness! Amen!

(Pope Pius XII)

Lord, forgive me!

Lord God, I am guilty in Your eyes, in my own and in those of the people You love.
I have become ensconced in a false world.
I have placed obstacles in my path and cannot go any farther.
I have squandered the goods that belong to the poor.
I have not given them the bread to which they have a right.
I have encountered people unworthily and treated them like objects.
I am not the person I should be.
Lord God, I am guilty in Your eyes, in my own and in those of the people You love.

(F. Anton Rotzetter)

Prayer of Blessing   (fourth century)

You are blessed, a blessing are you!

May the Lord be before you, to show you the right path. You are blessed, a blessing are you !

May the Lord be beside you, to embrace you and protect you. You are blessed, a blessing are you!

May the Lord be behind you, to catch you when you fall, to rescue you from the snare.
You are blessed, a blessing are you!

May the Lord be in you, to console you when you are sad. You are blessed, a blessing are you!

May the Lord be about you, to defend you when others attack you. May the Lord be above you, to bless you.

May the good Lord thus bless you.

Jesus be watching over you,
May He defend you!

Jesus be within you,
May He strengthen you!

Jesus be about you,
May He keep you!

Jesus be before you,
May He guide you!

Jesus be behind you,
May He protect you!

Jesus be above you,
May He bless you!

This is the Time of Grace

Prayer to the Most Holy Heart of Jesus

Most Holy Heart of Jesus, source of all goodness,
I worship You, I believe in You, I place my hope in You,
I love You and repent of all my sins.
I give You my poor heart; make it humble, patient and
pure and in every way as You would wish.
Grant, 0 merciful Jesus, that I live in You and You in me.
Protect me in all danger, console me in distress and sorrow.
Bestow upon me good health, Your blessing in all I do
and the grace of a holy death. Amen!

Prayer to give Joy to the Most Holy Heart of Jesus

0 Jesus, I love You so much!
Take me, take my whole being!
Guide me to You!

0 Jesus, I wish to be Your child.
In joy and in pain
Pray never leave me alone!

0 Jesus, I love You so much!
Take my heart, for I wish to share
Your great suffering!

0 Jesus, I love You so much!
Take from me everything that obstructs
My path to You! Amen!

This is the Time of Grace

Lord God, heal me from all ill

My Lord and creator,
You are God, who heals what is broken.
So much in my life is broken.

You know the story of my life
From the very beginning until today.
How often have I been bitterly disappointed!
How many of my hopes are dashed!
How much did I expect from life,
Yet how little has been fulfilled.

How often was I discouraged!
How often was I hurt and offended!
Bad memories plague me;
Old wounds still pain me;
Bitterness and grudges poison my soul.

Help me to forgive!
Almighty God, You are my refuge.
You alone are holy and You are the source
Of all holiness; absolve me and heal me!

Act of Dedication to the Immaculate Heart of Mary

Hail Mary, Queen of Peace, Blessed Mother of our Lord and Saviour Jesus Christ!

We wish humbly to unite our imperfect hearts with your Immaculate Heart, O Mother, cradle of godly mercy, thus renewing the vows of our Baptism. We promise to strive for the daily conversion your Son advises and to renounce worldly compromises.

Confident of your motherly protection and mediation, we wish to be true witnesses of God's love in our time, always under the guidance of the Holy Father as your Son's representative an earth.

With childlike obedience to your loving recommendations, we wish to gain the strength to follow Jesus devotedly, through frequent confession, communion and prayer, especially the Rosary. We are prepared to make sacrifices and to practise renunciation.

We know you are with us, 0 heavenly Mother. With gratitude and joy, we respond to your motherly exhortation to appreciate the grace of our time and to live in accordance with God's will. We, in turn, wish to give you joy. We join with your Immaculate Heart in striving to have as many souls as possible chosen to spend eternity with you and your beloved Son in Paradise.

This is the Time of Grace

Appendix

**Heavenly Father, bless me!
I commit my life into Your hands!
You can take it; You are the one who gave it!
Bless me in life and in death!
Father, I laud You!**

(Theodor Korner)

The only true future is the life eternal!

(Charles de Foucauld)

Christmas

Festival of Joyous Hope

Christmas is the holy day of the family. It is the celebration day of joy, peace, spiritual contentedness and true happiness! Immanuel ('God with us') comes to be with us and this is repeated again and again. The word 'Christmas' is, nevertheless, always moving, exciting, solemn and joyous. It is almost as if there were no word lovelier than this. The message of Christmas inspires us anew every time!

Even the thought of this great celebration day fills our soul with a special kind of tenderness and holiness. It warms our minds with gladness and light and fills our hearts with joy, kindness and peace. Here we find the meaningfulness that our life somehow focuses on as its goal. Something in the soul is lit up, so to speak, and it is so moving that it can hardly be expressed in words. When we feel such happiness, we simply wish it could continue always and into eternity. That is why true Christmas is so dear to us. We might almost say we could not imagine life without Christmas. Every year we wait for it again with mystical delight. For days, for months or even the whole year, people await Christmas. It is the great celebration day we live for until it arrives and the one we live on when it has passed.

Christmas is the holy day when godly love came down to us humans. It is the celebration day of life, of joyful hope, of the child, of great yet humble God, of the family, of peace…. God, who is eternal love, came here as our Brother and did so without ceasing to be God. Is there anything more amazing, more delightful and more wonderful than this truth? 'And the Word became flesh and

This is the Time of Grace

dwelt among us!' (John 1, 14) The glad tidings are exactly that. Therefore we sing with the angels who sang at His birth: 'Glory to God in the highest and on earth peace among men with whom He is pleased!' (cf. Luke 2, 14) 'For to us a child is born, to us a son is given; and the government will be upon His shoulder; and His name will be "Wonderful Counsellor, Mighty God, Everlasting Father, Prince of Peace".' (Isaiah 9, 6)

The Son of God taking on flesh, becoming a human being among us through the Holy Spirit in accordance with God's will, is an extraordinary and miraculous event. It is a mystery of our faith, one we believe in and live by. What would be impossible for God to do, if He chose to? Though the Lord God knows everything and always did know everything and always will do so, including how we feel in the trials of our life on earth, He can no longer be (unfairly) reproached with sovereign or unfeeling observation of our life from above. This reproach was always one that is unjustified; God is love! He wanted to demonstrate His love by His coming to earth as one of us. We can finally be convinced that He truly understands us. We can trust Him and tell Him everything, even complain if necessary. He will gladly listen and console us and help us better than any person. He will give us His peace and joy, even in the midst of our difficulties.

We may wonder why God was so humble as to come to earth as a little child. Everyone loves a little child and a little child loves everyone. Jesus was born for us and lived in order to win salvation for us. He came to teach us, to recommend an ideal way of life to us and to show us how to attain eternal happiness. He healed the sick and drove out demons; He did not keep this power only for Himself but allowed others to share it. Jesus was the perfect and unique example to us!

Christmas, the fulfilment of what mankind longs for:

Through Christmas we have come to understand better who God is: goodness itself, grace so sublime that we cannot imagine it, eternal love.... Who, then, is man, who this loving God created? He created mankind in His own image. It follows that, the creation being a masterpiece of God, mankind is the crown. With the coming of the divine child at Christmas, man was again able to attain grace and blessed immortality. For many centuries, even millennia, before that, mankind had been an outcast, having rejected God's grace and fallen into sin. Mankind had sought happiness without God and had paid dearly for it. Arrogance, disobedience and impurity are the opposite of God and God's love; where the former are, God cannot remain. After man's fall from grace, he began to stumble and strayed ever farther away from God. His isolation and wretchedness led God to take pity on him and offer him forgiveness; no being is more merciful than God. He decided to send us His own Son, His other self, to restore friendship between the mighty God that He is and mankind. Thus, His love overflowed and came to earth in the light of heavenly glory one wintry night in Bethlehem, amid the sighs and longing of mankind for restoration to the state of grace. This was the first Christmas. There is no greater gift God could have given us than His Son.

There is still no greater gift that He could give us: God is in His Son, Jesus Christ, and Jesus is in God, the eternal Father. The gift of God to us is the gift of Himself, in the form of Jesus, who dwelt among us and brought us the era of salvation. It is said, and rightly, that Jesus, by His birth, cut the history of humanity in two, namely, the time in which humanity longingly awaited God and the time in which God longingly awaits humanity. In fact, they both long for one another at any time. As Fenelon says, if we remove the Bethlehem crib, history has a terrible void. In the light of Christ's birth, all our sufferings become meaningful. They change into a way that leads us to an encounter with Him, the living God.

Our response to Christmas:

We owe Jesus, at every Christmas, an appropriate response to His coming and His love. As Otto Karrer says, "What use would it be if Jesus were to be born a thousand times in Bethlehem and we were to sing our carols to Him a thousand times and call out His holy name just as often, without living in His love, without helping and loving others as He did but were just to lead our own selfish lives?" Have we prepared ourselves to receive Jesus? Would we not make preparations to receive a king? Jesus is King, in the form of a little child who would like to be born deep in our hearts. If we die to sin and begin a new life, this will surely happen. Let Him live in us and in all we do. Let Him work with our hands and our heart when we work; let Him speak when we speak; let Him go with us wherever we go; let Him be with us in our pain and in our joy. He will be born in us when we start to see in each of our fellows a true brother or sister and also the child of Bethlehem. He Himself said, 'Truly, I say to you, as you did to one of the least of these my brethren, you did to Me.' (Matt. 25, 40) The Christmas message for God's people will always be: "Receive Jesus, be good and love one another as Jesus loved you!" Where people revere truth, love, freedom and peace, there Jesus will be. May He help us to remain in faith, hope and love of others and to bring His peace to all our fellow beings. May it be so now and to our final meeting with Him in eternity.

The true story of a Christmas present:

The following event really took place, though it may sound like a fairy tale. On a cold evening in Zagreb, Croatia, a group of workers hurried through the snow to the railway station. Then they were all astounded to hear, very near them, the distressed crying of a tiny child. They jumped up from their seats, looked around and found a basket, all by itself, with a newborn baby lying in it on a soft pillow and carefully wrapped in a shawl.

They were deeply touched at the sight of the tiny, helpless little thing and wondered what to do. The train was due any moment. One of them said it would be best to ring the police. In all the confusion, there came a poor workman through the crowd, who took the child in his arms, put his warm coat around it and said, "Where nine children have enough to eat, a tenth will be filled too."

When Joseph, for that was his name, arrived home with the baby, his wife was more than a little surprised. He, however, said, "As long as you all have your Joseph to look after and love you all, you need not be worried about anything." Before he had finished speaking, his wife had already taken the child lovingly and now she began to wash and change it and to feed it. The other nine children looked joyfully on as it slept. Their father said, "Children, Christmas will be here soon but for us Jesus was born today. This is Jesus! He is in our midst. We need not make a crib now. All we need is the Christmas tree."

The next morning, Joseph went to work and all but the tiny children to school. The mother, when changing her new child's bedding, found in the basket under the mattress a fat purse and a note which said: 'for the person who takes in my child'. The good woman was completely

This is the Time of Grace

overcome. In the evening she told her husband of the find. All he could say was, "How I thank You, dear Lord!"

Christian, for that was the name they had given the baby, grew into a fine, strong lad, wanting for nothing, among his brothers and sisters. He was loved and wanted and throughout the family there was harmony and peace. One day, Joseph told Christian how he had come to be a member of the family. At first, the boy was slightly confused; he went pale and wiped a few tears from his eyes but they were tears of gratitude! He said to Joseph, "You will always be my father!" His father felt like weeping too. As he grew up, Joseph gave him all the necessary attention and love. Christian loved him and was always grateful to his father. He finished school and completed his further studies most successfully.

Any time of the year, not only at Christmas, we can receive God's pure, boundless love into our heart and also pass it on to others. Every new moment we have the chance to do so. 'Whoever receives this child in my name receives Me, and whoever receives Me receives Him who sent Me.' (Luke 9, 48) Good thoughts, good words and good deeds open our hearts and purify them. Love is something we need not hesitate to give; the more we give it away, the more of it we end up having. Love is God and God is infinite.

Easter

Christ´s Gift of Love

In His death, He gave us salvation from death!
His resurrection was also resurrection for us!

(Preface)

Through His death, He annihilated our death!
With His resurrection, He restored our life to us!

Easter! It is the greatest, most moving and most important day in the long history of mankind and of Christianity. It is the holiest of all holy days.

Jesus Christ is risen! This sounds joyous and exciting, yet so solemn and petrifying too. Jesus Christ, true man and true God, accepted the torture and the humility of the cross. He died on the cross and was buried as a human corpse. There were hundreds, if not thousands of witnesses to His death. Then came the unfathomable miracle of His resurrection from the grave on the third day. He was alive again as flesh and blood, radiant and healthy! Who but God could achieve such a thing? Few had even dared to hope His prediction of His resurrection could come true.

This is the Time of Grace

The resurrection as the most fundamental tenet of our faith:

The Lord is risen; He is alive and is in our midst. He is immortal. Today, too, He offers us His peace and His joy. Is this not the most marvellous message still reverberating round the globe for over twenty centuries now? It plainly says that, although we will also be in our grave one day, our Lord will awaken us. He overcame the finality of human death for us, His children. No-one had been able to enter eternal Life with God before that.

There is no more basic tenet of our faith than this. Our faith can no more be destroyed than our Lord can. The greatest event reported in the Gospel is that God awakened His Son Jesus from the dead. (cf. 1 Thess. 1, 10) Then the apostles saw the Lord. (cf. John 20, 25)

Our faith is meaningful through the resurrection:

Our oldest testimony to the resurrection comes directly from St Paul, who emphasizes that it is his own. "For I delivered to you as of first importance what I also received, that Christ died for our sins in accordance with the scriptures, and that He appeared to Cephas, then to the twelve. Then He appeared to more than five hundred brethren at one time, most of whom are still alive, though some have fallen asleep. Then He appeared to James, then to all the apostles. Last of all, as to one untimely born, He appeared also to me." (1 Cor. 15, 3-8)

The Gospel reports graphically on the encounter of Christ resurrected with the apostles. His death on the cross had left them sad, disappointed and fearful. Suddenly, there appeared the Lord Jesus they had known so well for the previous three years. He is alive and in their midst. He is not only visible but He speaks to them, beginning with His customary greeting, 'Peace be with you!' He also eats with them. He invites Thomas to place a hand into His wound in His side and recommends that he not be unbelieving but believing. Even Thomas, the most sceptical of all, must believe the seemingly impossible.

Luke reports: "They were startled and frightened, and supposed that they saw a spirit. And He said to them, 'Why are you troubled, and why do questionings rise in your hearts? See My hands and My feet, that it is I Myself; handle me, and see; for a spirit has not flesh and bones as you see that I have.' " (Luke 24, 37-40)

St Paul writes of Jesus, "He is the head of the body, the Church; He is the beginning, the first-born from the dead, that in everything He might be pre-eminent. For in Him all the fullness of God was pleased to dwell, and through Him to reconcile to Himself all things, whether on earth or in Heaven, making peace by the blood of His cross." (Col. 1, 18-20) The apostle John writes, "... Jesus Christ, the faithful witness, the first-born of the dead, and the ruler of kings on earth." (Rev. 1, 5) Eternal life for us too is reality, even in Paradise; since Easter, we now have salvation. The apostle Matthew quotes Jesus as saying, "As for the resurrection of the dead, have you not read what was said to you by God, 'I am the God of Abraham, and the God of Isaac, and the God of Jacob'? He is not God of the dead, but of the living." (Matt. 22, 31-32) Every soul ever created is eternal but not every soul will spend eternity in bliss, in the presence of God, who is Life.

The celebration of the resurrection of Christ:

Jesus tells us He is the resurrection and the Life. If we believe in Him, we are worthy of eternal Life; we do as He commanded us and we belong to Him. This is the solution to the problems of our life. We know that this cross of our earthly life will end and we hope for resurrection in Him. We are required to renounce sin, to lead a worthy life, to be an example to others and to spread the Spirit of Christ beyond our own sphere, not least through prayer.

Does resurrected Jesus really live in us and we in Him? This depends on us! We can best answer this question with our lives! The more we live for God, the more moments there are that we turn into moments of grace. Thus Easter is renewed when we renew ourselves in its Spirit. It is worthwhile taking a few quiet moments to review our lives. Easter is not a ritual, one we simply repeat automatically every year. It is the victory of good over evil, love over hatred, forgiveness over revenge, joy over sadness,…. We need only make this victory, won for us through the shedding of His Most Precious Blood, the reality and the meaning of our lives. This is the path to eternal Paradise. Our life is now. This is the time of grace for the world, too.

Nobody asked you?

You say nobody asked you whether you wanted to be born.

You say nobody asked you what parents and brothers and sisters you wanted.

Nobody asked you...

but are you so sure no-one is there who knows everything and wanted it all to be that way;

and who wanted you just as you are, where you live and with those near you?

Are you really so sure no-one asked for you?

He not only asked for you, He loved you and He wanted you that way!

If you question your life and your own being, why do you not first ask HIM, the cause of all being?

Father Petar´s special task regarding the secrets:

If asked about the ten Medjugorje secrets, Father Petar confirms that he was chosen by the visionary Mirjana to announce each secret to the world three days before it occurs; at that point he is allowed to give us details of what will happen and where. He himself will only know of each secret ten days before its occurrence and he will spend the first seven days in prayer and fasting. The secrets will be written an a piece of parchment for him to read. At present, only the visionaries know when these events will take place.

The first two events concern Medjugorje and are warnings. The third will be a visible sign an the Mount of Apparitions. These events are meant to promote conversion and strengthen our faith.

Father Petar says our heavenly Mother has appeared so frequently in these last 150 years because the world has been in great danger. In Lourdes, she appeared in 1858 when moral liberalism was becoming a threat. In Fatima, she appeared in 1917 when the world was first threatened by Communism; this was the year of the Russian revolution. It is also the year in which the world accepted Einstein's theories, paving the way for atomic weapons; Our Lady warned us in Fatima of mass annihilation through weapons of destruction. In Medjugorje, she first appeared in 1981 and pleaded for peace, to lessen the tragic effects of the civil war which threatened the Balkan Peninsula and which finally broke out exactly ten years later.

the visionary Mirjana

The message of Our Lady to the world is that we should act urgently to save humanity and save our souls.

This is the Time of Grace